LEFTIES AREN'T LIMITED. JUST CHECK OUT
SOME OF THE MOST FAMOUS AND
REMARKABLE LEFT-HANDED PEOPLE
IN HISTORY:

Tom Cruise
Leonardo da Vinci
Albert Einstein
Benjamin Franklin
Whoopi Goldberg
Cary Grant
Ken Griffey Jr.
Paul McCartney
Michelangelo
Martina Navratilova
Julia Roberts
Oprah Winfrey

# Loving Lefties

*How to Raise* **Lefties**
*Your Left-Handed Child in a*
*Right-Handed World*

## Jane M. Healey, Ph.D.

Presented by LifeTime Media
352 Seventh Avenue
New York, NY 10001

POCKET BOOKS
New York  London  Toronto  Sydney  Singapore

An *Original* Publication of POCKET BOOKS

 POCKET BOOKS, a division of Simon & Schuster, Inc.
1230 Avenue of the Americas, New York, NY 10020

ISBN: 0-7434-0750-4

First Pocket Books trade paperback printing November 2001

10 9 8 7 6 5 4 3 2 1

POCKET and colophon are registered trademarks of Simon & Schuster, Inc.

For information regarding special discounts for bulk purchases, please contact Simon & Schuster Sales at 1-800-456-6798 or business@simonandschuster.com

Cover design by Tom McKeveny; front cover photo by PhotoDisc

Printed in the U.S.A.

*To my friend, Nancy,*

*my favorite lefty and partner in crime:*
*This book is for you. I hope you're watching.*

*Love,*
*Jane*

# Acknowledgments

I would like to thank my husband, Tony, and my lovely daughter, Lina, for their unfailing encouragement and support. I would also like to thank the people at LifeTime Media, Jacqueline Varoli and Karen Kelly, for helping to make this book possible. And a special thanks to my writer, Grant Jarrett, for so eloquently putting my thoughts and feelings into words.

# Contents

# Introduction

When I was a child, and throughout my teen years, I recognized that my left-handedness made me stand out. Although it was indeed frustrating at times, my foremost feeling during those years was that it somehow made me special. It interested me and appeared to interest many of those around me, particularly other left-handers. It's my experience that left-handers see themselves as a part of an exclusive club. Of course, most left-handers don't make a career out of their lateral preferences. They make the necessary adjustments and go about their lives without a lot of ballyhoo.

My initial interest in working with children developed when I interned at the City University of New York graduate school in the Albert Einstein College of Medicine, where I worked with Dr. Steve Mattis, and at the Columbia Presbyterian–Medical Center, where I worked with Drs. Rita Rudel and Martha Denckla. I would later do my first study of left-handedness in children with these two women. It was in college, however, that my youthful interest in handedness became a kind of fascination. Although I knew by then that I wanted to be a scientist, I didn't yet have a distinct focus. But while I was taking my first course in neuropsychology, I noticed that many of the studies of the left and right sides of the brain included a footnote stating that left-handers were excluded from the study because they were "different." This seemed more than a little peculiar to me, particularly in light of the fact that close to 40 percent of psychologists are left-handed. When I asked my professor why these studies insisted on excluding such a critical population and how we ever expected to learn anything about lateral preferences if they continued to do so, he suggested that I "calm down and write a paper on it." Of course that's exactly what I did. That term paper eventually expanded to become my doctoral dissertation.

Still, it wasn't until I was doing research at the Boston University School of Medicine that I became aware that scientists the world over were extremely interested in how and why lateral preferences came about and what set left-handers apart. In fact, there was a group of neuroscientists associated with the Aphasia Research Center who were virtually obsessed with the issue of left-handedness. These scientists, who were among the most supportive and encouraging I have ever known, demonstrated great respect for the researchers who were studying left-handedness.

I suppose it was only natural that I should bring my interest in and understanding of handedness into the field of child psychology. After all, I see many left- and mixed-handed children in my practice. Although I don't believe these children tend to have more problems than other children, I know that they do stand out. When left- or mixed-handed children have problems, they are often noticed more readily, but the great majority of the problems they experience are not a result of their hand-edness at all. As with right-handed children, the causes can be environmental, neurological, and even societal. And many of the issues that arise with lefties are simply the result of a lack of training and education on the subject. That, of course, is one of the reasons I decided to write this book.

So after leaving my friends and colleagues in Boston, I returned to New York, where for eleven years I was the director of the Child Psychology Division at the Mt. Sinai Medical Center. During that time, I trained numerous child psychologists and child neuropsychologists. I'm still an assistant professor at Mt. Sinai (as a volunteer faculty member), and I am currently an adjunct assistant professor in the Psychology Department at Fairleigh Dickinson University, Teaneck campus, where I teach child neuropsychology. I also maintain a private practice in child and adolescent neuropsychology at the Neuropsychology and Psychotherapy Center in Ridgewood, New Jersey, where I work with a wonderful group of professionals who, like me, live and breath child psychology. Feel free to contact us at (201) 251-8411 or (201) 444-8302. We'd love to hear from you!

With all of that going on, I guess I might have simply gone about my business without ever feeling compelled to write a book about left-handedness. But it just didn't sit right with me that a handful of scientists should be the only ones privy to this information—information that I firmly believe can be as crucial to our understanding of our children as information about any aspect of normal child development. There are literally dozens of books about ADD (attention deficit disorder) and numerous topics that affect far fewer people than the phenomenon of left-handedness.

There are a number of things that I hope I've accomplished in writing this book. I'd like to believe that in approaching this subject as a scientist, I've dispelled some of the many myths and misconceptions that have surrounded left-handedness for so long. I hope that by providing accurate and current information to parents, educators, and other child psychologists and neuropsychologists, I've helped to make everyone more aware of the issues left-handers can encounter and how to best handle them should they arise. And I'd like to think that this book will help to defuse unwarranted concerns—I don't feel it's too strong a statement to suggest that this book should be required reading for any parent who wants to have a better understanding of his or her left-handed children.

Most of all, I hope that I've shed some much-needed light on a subject that affects millions of children and adults every day, and that by doing so, I've begun the gradual process of shattering the obstacles that have too often impeded us in our efforts to understand and encourage one another. Only by understanding and encouraging our children can we help them to flourish and thrive. Onward.

Jane M. Healey, May 2001

# Chapter One

# Left-Handedness: A Brief Journey of Discovery

Imagine for a moment that you've landed on a planet meticulously designed to fit the needs of a privileged majority—a majority of which you are not a member. Then imagine that the difficulty you experience in trying to learn and master even the most fundamental skills is met with bewilderment, resistance, and anger. Add to that the natural human distrust of anything that differs from the norm and mix in the ample share of ridicule you are bound to receive from your peers. Oh yeah, and don't forget to throw in the emotional impact of your parents' and teachers' misguided efforts to "correct" your seemingly abnormal behavior. Getting uncomfortable? Well, we're not finished yet.

Imagine further that you are taught from the moment you land on this strange planet to ignore or struggle against your natural inclinations and that those few who take the time to attempt to teach you to use tools that were designed for them are, at best, unaware of the difficulties you're facing. Now imagine that it's not you we're talking about at all but your child.

Although this may sound overly dramatic, it was, not so long ago, an all-too-real depiction of the dilemma of the left-handed individual in an overwhelmingly right-handed society.

Fortunately, there have been dramatic changes in many areas. Many manufacturers now make left-handed versions of what were once problematic products, such as scissors, cameras, school desks, and certain musical instruments. Teachers, educators, occupational therapists, and child psychologists are becoming increasingly aware of laterality and the issues that are often related to it. There are Web sites, clubs, magazines, and shops devoted to all things left-handed, including fun and useful products and lists of successful lefties in virtually every field. Plus, it seems as though something new is learned about the human brain every day. As a parent, the more you know about your left-handed child, the better off both of you will be. And there is so much to learn about your precious lefty!

Although the situation is improving, there is still a lot of work to be done. There are still many people who don't recognize the different needs and strengths of left- versus right-handers—parents, teachers, coaches, and even therapists who are frustrated or concerned because they don't understand why a child is having difficulty with one area or another. In spite of the shelves full of books about virtually every other aspect of child rearing, far too many parents and educators remain uneducated about this important aspect of their children's lives.

But before we get back to the future, let's take a look at where we've come from.

## Myths and Misconceptions Debunked

Throughout recorded history, left-handers the world over have been the objects of scorn and fear. They have been characterized as outcasts, degenerates, and communists and perceived as inferior, clumsy, unlucky, sinister, and even satanic (the Latin term for left-handedness is *sinistral*). The devil is most often depicted as being left-handed, and in Buddhism the road to Nirvana is said to split into two paths: the left, or "the wrong way," and the right, or the "path to enlightenment." In the earliest plays, the villains always entered from the left side of the stage.

In the 1600s, in both Europe and the American colonies, women accused of witchcraft were publicly stripped and examined. Moles or blemishes found on the left side of the body of an accused witch were considered absolute proof of guilt. This may sound ridiculous today, but it is part of a deep-rooted tradition. English writer and political philosopher H. G. Wells, author of *The Time Machine* and *The War of the*

*Worlds*, believed the left side of the brain was larger than the right—a theory long since proven incorrect. Actually, we now know that some areas of the brain are larger on the right than on the left, and vice versa. For instance, the area on the left side of the brain that is responsible for processing speech is larger than the equivalent area on the right.

In the 1800s and early 1900s, left-handed children were often beaten until they learned to use their right hands. And in some African and Asian cultures, the left hand is still considered the "dirty" hand because of its function in personal hygiene. It is not easy to struggle against such long-standing traditions.

The custom of buttoning women's clothing on the opposite side of men's is a holdover from the Victorian age, when pampered noblewomen were dressed by their right-handed maids. And there are two divergent theories regarding the wearing of the wedding ring on the left hand. One ascribes the custom to the early Egyptians, who believed that despite the left hand's supposed flaws, placing the ring on this hand brought it nearer to the heart. Another attributes it to the Greeks and Romans, who purportedly wore the rings to ward off the evil associated with the left hand.

There have been a few rare exceptions to this pattern, such as the Incas, who revered left-handers, and the Zuni tribe, who believed left-handedness signified good luck. But even these seemingly positive views of the left hand are based on superstition and ancient ritual.

These days few people consciously regard others as

> The Incas revered left-handed people; the North American Zuni tribe believe left-handed people signify good luck.

evil or sinister on the basis of the hand they use to throw a ball or hold a pencil. There is little serious discussion of witchcraft, and thanks to hard science, we no longer have to guess about the size or weight of the brain.

Modern hygiene enables us to use both of our hands for any number of disparate activities without fretting about contamination or propriety. Most women now button their own clothes—we seem to have adjusted to the vestigial configuration of buttons quite well. And the tradition of wearing a wedding ring has outlived the myths that brought it about.

But although most of these myths have been dispelled, there has been some carryover, both in our attitudes and in our language.

## The "Right" Language

The subtler expressions of our prejudices, those we are unaware of, are often the most insidious. These prejudices are deeply imbedded in our language and are frequently expressed without a second thought. A left-handed compliment is one that carries with it a negative message; if you are described as having two left feet, you are probably not going to win the Saturday-night tango contest. But right is . . . well, it's right. What more could anyone possibly want than to be right? Right?

The French word for left-handedness is *gauche*, which also means "awkward," "clumsy," or "lacking social polish." In German, *links*, the term for left, also means "awkward." The Italian word for left-handed, *mancini*, means "crooked" or "deformed." The Portuguese term for left, *canhoto*, means feeble or weak.

For some reason, evil spirits tend to reside over the left shoulder (and have a strong aversion to airborne salt). Pouring wine with the left hand is believed to bring bad luck, and a left-handed toast is said to be insincere or malevolent.

In the Australian slang expression for left-handedness, *molly-dooker*, *molly* is slang for a young woman and *dooker* is slang for one who fights with the fists, whereas in the comparable English expression *cack-handed*, *cack* is defined as excrement. For some, even the relatively benign term *southpaw*, a term originally coined to describe left-handed pitchers, may be insulting. If this doesn't seem to make sense, think for a moment of how up in arms you would be if these epithets were used to describe your race or religion.

## Frustrations: sdrawkcaB sI dlroW yM

Scissors, cameras, tools, and musical instruments are among the list of everyday items that have traditionally been designed for the right-handed majority. Left-

> Writing left-handed is not the opposite of writing right-handed; the two actions are completely different.

handed writing, if not taught by teachers sensitive to the way lefties do things, can be deeply frustrating and occasionally humiliating (more on this later).

Playing cards are difficult to read, and power saws are dangerous, if not impossible to use. Apple corers and potato peelers are major annoyances, and attempting to use a standard can opener can tie your fingers up in knots.

As you can see, a great profusion of tools and activities have been neatly fashioned for the comfort and convenience of right-handers. If you're a member of the right-handed majority, this is a perfect time to try a little experiment. Strap your wristwatch to your right wrist and then try to adjust the time. Clumsy? Hmmm.

That's not because your left hand is not your dominant hand; it is because the crown is thoughtfully positioned on the right side of the watch to make it easily accessible to a right-handed person.

If you're still harboring doubts, take a standard pair of scissors in your left hand, a sheet of newspaper in your right, and do some snipping. Frustrating, isn't it?

Again, it isn't your lateral preference that's stifling you; it's the design of the scissors. Who wouldn't appear clumsy when fighting the laws of physics? Who wouldn't feel a blow to confidence, and, in time, self-esteem? All of this can be magnified in childhood, particularly when your peers, who have been given the same tools to work with, appear to be so effortlessly competent.

One thing parenting experts and parents agree on is the importance of self-esteem. Children learn very early who they are. Numerous studies prove it, and logic and experience confirm that how you feel about yourself will play a significant role in determining your behavior now and in the future.

If you are a parent or plan to be one, you've probably already studied and made educated decisions regarding everything from what to eat when trying to conceive to breast-feeding to "normal" developmental milestones to college funds. The critical issue of lateral preferences deserves the same level of commitment. Simply put, by learning about handedness, you can help fortify your child's emotional well-being.

We spend hundreds of thousands of dollars on toys made to promote and foster brain development. We play Mozart and engage in all sorts of games and activities hoping to stimulate our children's minds. We learn the guidelines of normal motor development, but we are uneducated on the subject of handedness.

As parents, or parents-to-be, you have the opportunity and the responsibility to make your child's journey a pleasant and fruitful one, and to make this occasionally hostile planet more accommodating to its left-handed children. By educating yourself and by learning how to determine and support your child's natural lateral preferences, you can offer him or her a brighter future and help dispel the myths and misconceptions we've all been burdened with for far too long.

## The Good News

There is far more good news than bad about being left-handed. The long-standing prejudices are slowly being stripped of their power by logic and science, and there are new products available every day. Many left-handed children may never perceive their handedness as a problem; on the contrary, they will view themselves as special. And this is as it should be. Lefties are part of a special club, and we don't really mind when we are inconvenienced—we simply take it in stride.

In fact, substantial evidence shows that left-handers can and do enjoy healthy, happy lives, unfettered by misinformation, undaunted by the very real obstacles they sometimes face. In addition to those lives, history is teeming with examples of creative, successful, powerful, and extraordinary left-handers. Actors, artists, musicians, world leaders, athletes, scientists, and writers fill the growing ranks. Each of the following chapters will feature a list of some of these left-handed luminaries.

---

Throughout history, there has been a plethora of left-handed geniuses, artists, and athletes: Albert Einstein, Leonardo da Vinci, Michelangelo, Babe Ruth.

---

# Chapter Two

## *Studies and Statistics*

The most recent statistics show that approximately 10 to 15 percent of the U.S. and British populations are left-handed—about 30 million people in the United States alone. Parents and grandparents of left-handers also number in the millions.

At an estimated 9 percent, people of Asian or Hispanic lineage are apparently slightly less likely to be left-handed. But determining accurate statistics in other cultures has proven a slow and difficult road. Because of the vestiges of ancient mythology and the biases that linger, studies of countries such as Africa and India are uncommon. However, very recent studies of hand preference in India show a decreased rate of left-handedness compared to the West. But this probably has little to do with the Western world's influence on other cultures and may instead be the result of a completely different gene pool.

Men are slightly more likely to be left-handed than women are. Though the reasons for this are not entirely clear, one prominent theory suggests elevated testosterone levels may play a part in left-handedness. Testosterone is a naturally produced hormone responsible for the development and maintenance of secondary male characteristics. This theory may explain the correlation that seems to exist between left-handedness and some immune disorders, as testosterone has also been linked to immune disorders.

Though the reasons remain unclear, some studies show that left-handedness is more common among twins and low-birth-weight babies. Interestingly, the fact that some identical twins do not share lateral preference seems to cast considerable doubt on the theories that advance genetics as the sole determinant of handedness.

According to several studies, young people are approximately twice as likely to be left-handed as the elderly. This may be due to the increasingly liberal attitudes about left-handedness. Although it was once commonplace to force a change in a child's lateral preference, the practice is far less widespread today.

Many studies have shown that the incidence of left-handedness seems to decrease with age. Dr. Chris McManus, a neuropsychologist who studies handedness, reviewed some of these studies and noted that left-handedness is roughly two times higher in 15-year-olds than in 70-year-olds. He proposes three explanations for this trend. First, today's reduced social pressure to change handedness may be a factor. Second, left-handers tend to conform to a right-handed society over time, which may make them more right-handed as they get older. Finally, Dr. McManus suggests that there is a changing gene frequency and that there may actually be more left-handed genes around now than in the past. He argues for the third explanation, that genes may be changing, at least in Western culture. We do not know the reason for this trend.

Numerous studies have shown a clear genetic link to lateral preference. According to studies by renowned British psychologist Marian Annett at Coventry Polytechnic in Lancaster, England, about 45 percent of children born to two left-handed parents are left-handed (or lean toward left-handedness). A little over half that number will be left-handed if only the mother is left-handed (about 25 percent), and about 20 percent will be left-handed if only the father is left-handed. According to Annett's "right shift" genetic theory of handedness, about 50 percent of the children of two left-handed parents should be left-handed or predominantly left-handed. So why are only 45 percent left-handed? The reason, according to Annett, is that there is still some

Left-handedness runs in families. Lefties in the British royal family include the Queen Mother, Queen Elizabeth II, Prince Charles, and Prince William.

cultural bias or pressure toward right-handedness, so that if a child is only leaning slightly toward left-handedness, the parents may reward right-handed behaviors. Consequently, some of the children who might have been lefties turn out to be righties.

The conclusions these studies lead to are certainly interesting, but they are clearly contingent on how you choose to assess and define left-handedness. Although many left-handers are exclusively left-handed, a segment of the population in question has varying degrees of left-handedness. There are those who write, draw, eat, and brush their teeth with their left hands but who point and throw baseballs with their right. In fact, it is believed that there are at least two subgroups of left-handers: those who are consistently left-handed for most skilled activities and those who are inconsistently left-handed.

There is also a small population of people who are considered ambidextrous, which means that they are equally comfortable using either hand for most tasks. This phenomenon is relatively rare—recent studies show that only about 1 in 200 people is truly ambidextrous.

Depending on how many tasks and activities you consider in a study, and which ones you choose, the potential variety of combinations is almost unlimited. In studies that consider only those who use their left hands

---

Fifteen percent of right-handed people use their left hand for major activities, such as throwing a ball, batting, and ironing.

---

"exclusively" to be left-handed, the numbers will be lower than in those that include people who demonstrate lesser degrees of left-handedness or those who are not strictly right-handed. Degrees of dominance are generally determined by assessing preference and/or proficiency in a predetermined set of skills. Unfortunately, different studies use different guidelines. The absence of a single protocol makes accurate numbers extremely difficult to sort out.

I completed a large-scale study of hand preferences in a university population with my colleague, Boston University psychologist Jackie Liederman. We found numerous variations in hand preference, even in right-handers. We found that there were different preferences for different sets of activities, like sports or fine motor activities. We concluded that handedness is multidimensional and *very* complicated!

If this all sounds unnecessarily confusing, well . . . it probably is. Even prominent researchers in the field can't seem to figure us lefties out! Dr. Michael Corballis, a psychologist at the University of Auckland who has been involved in the study of left-handedness for close to 30 years, summarized a recent symposium on left-handedness this way: "Left-handedness has been around for a long time, yet we still don't fully understand it." He notes that we have known for a long time that left-handedness is partially genetic, yet we haven't even come close to finding the responsible gene. Fortunately, there is another way to look at it. Here are some basic facts:

1. It is safe to assume that at least one in ten people is left-handed.
2. *One in ten* means that around 30 million people in the United States are lefties.
3. A little more than half of the 30 million are boys.
4. The percentage of lefties is slightly lower among Asians and Hispanics.
5. Those under age 10 are more likely to be left-handed than those over age 65.
6. Having one left-handed parent increases your chances of being left-handed.
7. Having two left-handed parents increases your chances further.
8. Being a twin may increase your chances of being left-handed.
9. You and your twin may not share lateral preferences.
10. Test procedures are often imperfect. (This is a good thing to keep in mind regardless of the topic.)

## Modern Myths and Misconceptions

We have already discussed some of the mythology surrounding left-handedness, but not all of this mythology has its roots in ancient history. There are also a number of modern misconceptions.

Some people believe that dominance should always be on the same side of the body. But there is no evidence to support that theory. In fact, many children, right- or left-handed, do not have dominance all on the same side. We also now know that forcing a change in brain dominance can lead to other problems. Dominance is simply the side or area of the brain that commands most activities.

For example, there is evidence that children whose handedness has been switched have difficulty distinguishing left from right, and sometimes have spatial orientation problems.

There is also evidence that attempting to change your child's lateral preference, or handedness, can lead to stuttering, though this is less clear. It is possible that left- and mixed-handed children may be more prone to stuttering to begin with, because one side of the brain does not take total control of speech; therefore, the brain signals get confused. Attempting to switch their handedness may make matters worse.

What is certain is that trying to make a child all right-sided or all left-sided is not going to help him or her. He or she won't be more coordinated or read at a higher level. A child's brain is wired from birth to be a particular way. Certainly, we can help children become more coordinated, but switching their handedness is not the way to do it.

> The left hemisphere of the brain controls the motor coordination in righties, and the right hemisphere controls it in lefties.

People have speculated about the connection between mixed lateral preferences and emotional control, linking the "neurological disorganization" of having the dominant eye, hand, ear, and foot on different sides of the body with an inner emotional disorganization. They claim that people with mixed lateral preferences have a higher incidence of emotional outbursts, temper tantrums, and illogical behavior.

But recent studies indicate that the same types of in utero brain damage that can cause an inclination toward mental retardation and a whole host of developmental problems can also have an impact on the child's genetically determined lateral preferences, or handedness. These individuals are not genetic left-handers; they are, instead, the victims of in utero brain damage that has altered their natural or genetic lateral preference. This type of brain damage can often cause otherwise unrelated behavioral problems.

Further, we now know that lateral preferences for hand and eye aren't highly correlated. Most scientists and educators once assumed that handedness and eyedness should always be on the same side of the body. Stanley Coren, an eminent experimental psychologist at the University of British Columbia in Vancouver, Canada, discovered many years ago that this is not the case. Almost half of left-handers are right-eyed, and about one third of right-handers are left-eyed. Interestingly, handedness is more often correlated with footedness—the foot you prefer to kick with.

Eyedness refers to the dominant eye, the eye one sights with. This is different from acuity. To test for eye dominance, you can use the pointing technique. Point to an object in the distance, keeping both eyes open. For example, stand and point to a doorknob. Then close one eye and note whether your finger moves or stays directly aligned with the object. Then do the same with your other eye. Your dominant eye is the one that is open when your finger is directly lined up with the object you are sighting.

Dr. Coren was also one of the first researchers to look at age trends in handedness. Interestingly, instead of determining that the pressure to conform to a right-handed society has helped to decrease left-handedness with increasing age, he has suggested that left-handers simply die younger than right-handers. He explains that part of the reason for this is that heavy machinery such as that used in construction is made for right-handers, so the risk of accidents is higher for lefties. He also discusses the possibility that birth stress leads to brain damage and that this is more likely to happen to left-handers than to right-handers. He also notes the fact that lefties often have more allergies and asthma—another possible cause of early death. Though Dr. Coren's studies are substantial, the fact that elderly left-handers were forced to switch their lateral preferences early in life is undoubtedly a major reason for the deficit of left-handers in this age group.

Thanks to today's increasing awareness and understanding of handedness issues, parents and educators are slowly breaking through the myths and learning that encouraging their children's natural lateral preferences will help them to grow, learn, and live with much greater ease.

## What You Can Do

Your behavior as a parent during the earliest years of your child's development, and your understanding of his or her lateral preferences, can have significant long-term implications. You would never knowingly subject your son to extreme temperatures, and you wouldn't put glasses on a daughter who didn't require them, nor would you force your own custom-tailored diet on a newborn. Your overriding desire as a loving parent is undoubtedly to fulfill your child's needs and, when it is in his or her best interests, to accommodate any reasonable desires.

I believe that by educating yourself about lateral preferences, by taking the time and exerting the energy required to determine your child's own natural propensities, and by offering your love and support, you can make a potentially bumpy road smoother.

An open mind is a great place to start. And taking the time to observe your son or daughter performing various tasks is critical. Watch when he or she points. When you are handing him or her a spoon or a toy, place it in whichever hand is extended, in spite of your own instincts. Take the time to observe his or her proficiency in picking up Cheerios or slices of fruit. And above all, don't try to steer your child one way or the other. Let nature take its course, gradually.

If it turns out that you are indeed rearing a lefty, there are numerous steps you can take to facilitate his or her inclination. Left-handed children's scissors, pencil grips, rulers, and a variety of other home and school products designed to make daily life a little less frustrating are now readily available no matter where you live. You can alert your child's caretakers and teachers, and you can become involved at school to ensure that his or her special needs are accommodated. Furthermore, you can make your home environment lefty friendly and take steps to reduce the risk of accidents and injury.

Armed with knowledge, patience, understanding, and love, you can take an active part in your child's development and growth. You can help secure your child's chances for a successful and happy future.

## Famous Lefties

- Edwin "Buzz" Aldrin, astronaut
- Lord Baden-Powell, founder of the Boy Scouts (ambidextrous)
- F. Lee Bailey, lawyer
- Cecil Beaton, photographer and costume designer
- Lenny Bruce, comedian
- Milt Caniff, cartoonist
- Fidel Castro, Cuban leader
- Marcia Clark, lawyer
- Nicole d'Oresme, mathematician
- Albert Einstein, physicist (This is controversial.)
- Henry Ford, automobile manufacturer
- N. B. Forrest, Confederate general

- Alan Funt, television producer
- Uri Geller, psychokinetic performer
- Euell Gibbons, naturalist
- Matt Groening, cartoonist
- Cathy Guisewite, cartoonist
- John Wesley Harding, Western gunslinger
- Joel Hodgson, host of *Mystery Science Theater 3000*
- Helen Keller, advocate for the blind
- Jay Leno, comedian
- Allen Ludden, game-show host
- Benjamin Netanyahu, Israeli prime minister
- Pat Oliphant, political cartoonist
- August Piccard, explorer of the stratosphere and inventor of the bathyscape
- Paul Prudhomme, chef
- Pat Robertson, evangelist and politician
- David Rockefeller, banker
- Wally Schirra, astronaut
- General H. Norman Schwarzkopf, military man
- Dr. Albert Schweitzer, physician and missionary
- Dr. Mark Silver, surgeon
- Richard Simmons, exercise guru
- Bart Simpson, cartoon character

# Chapter Three

# How to Know If You're Raising a Lefty: Early Signs and Signals

I hope you now have a fundamental understanding of what it means to be left-handed. You have a grasp of the basic facts, and you've absorbed some of the statistics. You've come to understand the crucial role you can play in your child's development, and you've made a commitment to do everything in your power to facilitate his or her individual journey. You recognize how important the issue is, but you don't yet know how to recognize your child's lateral preferences.

Lateral preferences develop gradually as a child develops motor proficiency. Very often this development is not linear or straightforward. It's a little more compli-

Studies suggest that children who have one or two left-handed parents alternate between their right and left hands before developing a consistent hand preference.

cated than that. A child may use both hands for a period of time and then suddenly start using one of them more frequently for one particular activity.

My own daughter did this with eating. For a while, she consistently used her left hand to eat, but when she began to learn to throw a ball and perform other, more sophisticated tasks, she began using her right hand more. When she started to color, she switched back and forth between her hands but seemed to prefer her right hand. Throughout this crucial stage I watched her carefully and tried not to influence her behavior. I knew that she had about a 25 percent chance of using her left hand to write because I am left-handed. As she became more proficient, she used the right hand more and more, but she still continued to eat and do some other tasks with her left. Finally, she began using her right hand for eating too. However, she continues to favor her left foot for hopping and kicking.

There is evidence that children who have one or two left-handed parents are more likely to switch back and forth before they develop a consistent hand preference. There are two reasons for this: One is environmental—they are most likely following the unconscious and

Ultrasound shows that even in the womb, 90 percent of babies appear to favor their right thumb, and this corresponds to population breakdowns of righties and lefties.

inconsistent lead of those around them; the other is genetic. In fact, some of them never develop a consistent preference, because handedness is partially genetic. The evidence suggests that there is a right-handedness gene but no left-handedness gene. If you inherit a right-handedness gene, you will almost always be right-handed (it's dominant), but if you don't inherit a right-handedness or "right shift" gene, your handedness is free to vary in either direction or remain in between.

This is the crux of Marian Annett's genetic theory of handedness, which is still the most popular and useful theory we have. She calls the gene the "right shift factor." If you do not have this gene, your chances of being right-handed or mostly right-handed are approximately equal to those of being left-handed or predominantly left-handed. In other words, you can go in either direction, depending on where your environment takes you and how you are influenced. Many children who lack the right-handed gene ultimately become mixed-handed, which means they will use their left hand for some activities and their right hand for others. Often, this will remain the case for the rest of their lives.

This lack of right-handed gene explains why you

often see certain families with a lot of left- and mixed-handed individuals in them. Some of the family members are strongly left-handed, some right-handed, but many are mixed-handed. I see many families like this in my practice, and their dynamics are very interesting.

## Instinct and Environment

Although the age at which children begin to reveal their lateral preferences varies dramatically from child to child, the first clear indications generally appear between age 12 months and 5 years, with the average being age 3 years. Girls usually develop their hand preferences much earlier than boys, as much as 2 years earlier in some cases. When a girl uses her left hand consistently for many activities at the age of 2 years, you can be fairly certain she will be a lefty. But if a boy does the same thing, you can't be sure he won't switch over to the right at some point.

Children begin to use their hands almost immediately. They spread their fingers and clutch at any object within reach. They pull objects toward them and they push

It's not until around the age of 3 years that a child definitively expresses her hand preference by consistently using one hand over another for major activities like eating and playing.

them away—very often, onto the floor. One of the first habits most children develop is sucking their thumbs. Other early uses of the hands include waving, pointing, and manipulating toys and other objects.

When children first become mobile, they must use their hands as well as their feet to drag themselves across the floor, and later, when they want to stand, they use their hands to pull themselves up. They learn to hold their bottles before they learn to speak, and they use their hands to examine their own growing bodies as well as the intriguing world around them.

Children also mimic their parents and siblings. And they respond to input, whether subtle or manifest. If you force a child to consistently take his or her bottle in a particular hand or to use that one hand to hold his or her fork, you may be causing the child to struggle against a natural instinct. As discussed earlier, this can lead to frustration, clumsiness, and a multitude of other consequences.

Although you can't be expected to suddenly alter your natural behavior, you can be conscious of how your behavior affects your children. It may be perfectly natural for you to place a toy, a bottle, or a spoon in your child's right hand, but it may not be natural for him or her to receive it that way. The best bet is to place objects near the center of your child's body and allow him or her to reach for them. And remember that particularly in the earlier stages of development, the hand your child proffers will likely change from day to day. In some ways you are learning together.

# An Ill-Conceived and Outdated System

The problem with the tests that are most often used to determine a child's lateral preferences is that they weren't designed for children. Here are a few examples of the types of questions commonly used in these tests:

## Sample One

Which hand do you use for the following tasks? Please indicate *right* or *left*.

1. Writing
2. Holding a hammer
3. Inserting a key into a lock
4. Brushing your teeth
5. Using scissors

In this case, the candidate is asked only to answer *left* or *right* to each of five tasks. Consistency and degree of proficiency are not even addressed. A toddler will not yet have developed enough comfort with any of the activities to give an accurate response. The results derived from such a test are incomplete at best.

## Sample Two

Rank your hand preference for the following tasks:

1. Writing
   a. Comfortable only with my right hand

    b. Equally comfortable using either hand

    c. Comfortable only with my left hand

2. Carrying a heavy suitcase
   a. Comfortable only with my right hand
   b. Equally comfortable using either hand
   c. Comfortable only with my left hand

3. Swinging a baseball bat
   a. Comfortable only with my right hand
   b. Equally comfortable using either hand
   c. Comfortable only with my left hand

4. Holding a tennis racket
   a. Comfortable only with my right hand
   b. Equally comfortable using either hand
   c. Comfortable only with my left hand

5. Holding a hammer
   a. Comfortable only with my right hand
   b. Equally comfortable using either hand
   c. Comfortable only with my left hand

Although this test allows for some variance in degrees of proficiency and the prospect of dual-handedness, it deals mostly with gross motor skills, those that we now know show only one type of hand preference.

**Sample Three**

Please rate your degree of hand preference for the following tasks:

1. Writing
   a. Always use my right hand
   b. Prefer to use my right hand
   c. Am equally comfortable with either hand
   d. Prefer to use my left hand
   e. Always use my left hand

2. Using tweezers
   a. Always use my right hand
   b. Prefer to use my right hand
   c. Am equally comfortable with either hand
   d. Prefer to use my left hand
   e. Always use my left hand

3. Combing hair
   a. Always use my right hand
   b. Prefer to use my right hand
   c. Am equally comfortable with either hand
   d. Prefer to use my left hand
   e. Always use my left hand

4. Sewing or threading a needle (Which hand holds the thread?)
   a. Always use my right hand
   b. Prefer to use my right hand
   c. Am equally comfortable with either hand
   d. Prefer to use my left hand
   e. Always use my left hand

5. Holding a spoon
   a. Always use my right hand
   b. Prefer to use my right hand

c. Am equally comfortable with either hand
d. Prefer to use my left hand
e. Always use my left hand

The above questionnaire is far superior to the other examples because it covers a broader spectrum of preference, and it addresses some of the fine motor and practiced skills. But although it's perfectly appropriate for assessing basic handedness in older children, it won't be of much use in determining your 1-year-old's handedness. Obviously, young children have simply not yet had time to develop proficiency in these skills.

## Some Specific Indicators for Your Toddler

So how do you know if you are raising a lefty? First, look at your family's hand preferences, because that will be a large predictor of where the child will go. If both parents are righties, chances are about 10 to 12 percent that their child will be a lefty. If Mom is a lefty, chances increase to about 25 percent, and if both Mom and Dad are lefties, chances are closer to 50 percent.

---

Right-handed babies, when placed on their tummies, tend to turn their heads to the right. Lefties usually turn their heads to the left or don't show any preference at all.

---

Then take the time to watch your child's handedness gradually evolve. If you are already keeping a diary, add a section where you can keep track of your observations. If you're not yet doing this, now would be a great time to start. A diary of your child's development is something you will always cherish.

Scribbling and drawing are commonly accepted as an early indicator of a toddler's handedness. A child who grips crayons or other writing or drawing implements with a particular hand a majority of the time may be subconsciously communicating a natural inclination. But because it takes time for children to grow comfortable with the world around them, they will generally switch back and forth between their hands until they begin to develop a certain degree of comfort and proficiency with each individual skill. And remember, judging handedness by only one or two skills isn't the most reliable way to determine your child's handedness.

An observant parent can, however, look for other signs. For instance, children love to point and wave. Make note of which hand your child most often employs. Eating, a very regular task that is easy to observe, is also a fairly reliable early indicator. (In certain countries, it is customary to use a fork and knife in the right hand.) Picking up toys or other objects is another area where by simply observing you might begin to identify a natural preference. But be careful not to jump to conclusions. Some children will pick up a crayon in one hand, scribble for a while, and then switch. See which hand your child uses first and for the longest period of time.

Other common behaviors that bear scrutiny are:

- Holding a bottle or pacifier
- Finger painting
- Gripping a favorite doll or stuffed animal
- Rolling and later throwing a ball
- Swinging a bat or club
- Using toy tools, such as hammers and saws
- Playing with games that require some degree of dexterity, such as pegboards and toy telephones

Rather than approaching this as a quiz, make a list of the tasks and activities above and chart your child's preferences over a given period of time, noting each use of one hand or the other. For instance, you might try making a list of six or seven different tasks or activities. Each day for a week, choose a different one to focus on. In addition to how often each hand is used, make a note of which hand he or she begins with and which is used for a longer period of time. Depending on your patience, the consistency of the data, and whether your child has already developed a preference, you may be on your way to making a determination.

## An Active Role

Observation is by no means the only tool at your disposal. By practicing certain tasks with your child, such as throwing and catching a ball and drawing, you can help facilitate the development of his or her natural propensities. By exposing your child to a variety of gross and fine motor skills and allowing nature to take its gradual course, you will be participating in his or her development.

Remember, with any child, no matter what his or her lateral tendencies, it takes time to develop comfort with each task. Throwing a ball or beanbag overhand will follow throwing underhand, which will follow rolling or pushing the toy. Most children will use two hands before they switch to one, and their accuracy will take time to develop.

Whereas girls may be ready to work with crayons or markers before the age of 2 years, boys will probably be about a year behind—boys seem to like to keep their options open, whereas girls like to commit. Hmm. Be patient, don't expect too much too fast, and fight the urge to push your child one way or the other. In time, as your child's proficiency begins to increase, a natural preference will manifest itself, one that you and your child will have discovered together.

## Lefty U.S. Presidents

- James A. Garfield, twentieth
- Herbert Hoover, thirty-first
- Harry S. Truman, thirty-third
- Gerald Ford, thirty-eighth
- Ronald Reagan, fortieth
- George H. W. Bush, forty-first
- Bill Clinton, forty-second

# Chapter Four

## *The Biology and Physiology of Left-Handedness*

The brain is divided into two halves, known as cerebral hemispheres. At the base of the fissure that divides them is the corpus callosum, a bundle of nerve fibers that provide a communication link between the hemispheres. To the untrained eye, the right and left hemispheres appear to mirror one another, but there are significant functional distinctions between them.

Because of a crossing of the nerve fibers in the medulla, the lowermost portion of the brain, the left hemisphere controls the right half of the body, and the right hemisphere controls the left. Furthermore, although there is some diversion from the norm, in the majority of people the left hemisphere controls speech and language functions (including reading and writing), logic, reasoning, and motor programming, whereas the right hemisphere generally governs spatial perceptions, musical and artistic skills, faces, and emotions. Interestingly, visual processes, hearing, and mathematics are commonly shared between the two halves.

*Lateralization* refers to the degree to which each hemisphere is specialized for certain types of functions or processes. People differ greatly with respect to their lateralization patterns; some have strict lateralization of functions (language on the left, etc.), whereas others have a lesser degree of lateralization. When one cerebral hemisphere guides the other in a particular function, it is known as cerebral or hemispheric dominance. In other words, people aren't dominated by one side or the other of their brain, as was once believed. Rather, particular areas of the brain guide (not rule) specific processes and activities. And the two halves of your brain are in constant communication, cooperating rather than working against one another—working as a unit.

Interestingly, we've learned most of what we know about the functions of the different hemispheres by studying stroke victims. If we know which side of the brain has been affected by a stroke, and we see which functions are still operating properly and which ones are not, we can make educated inferences regarding which side of the brain controls which functions.

We are greatly indebted to Drs. Harold Goodglass, Edith Kaplan, and Norman Geschwind, among many others, for much of what we now know about the brain. In the early 1960s, Drs. Goodglass and Geschwind helped to establish a neuropsychology training and research facility at the Boston VA Medical Center, where I later had the good fortune to do my postdoctoral training. I worked with Drs. Goodglass and Geschwind on the subject of cerebral dominance, and together we devised a handedness questionnaire that went far beyond what was normally used at that time. Although Dr. Geschwind suffered a fatal heart attack in 1985 at the age of 56, our research culminated in two papers on handedness that I wrote with Professor Jackie Liederman from Boston University. (Dr. Geschwind had already passed away.) These papers became influential in the field.

Dr. Geschwind was the first to notice that the two sides of the brain are not totally symmetrical. He observed that the area of the brain known as Sylvus' fissure is longer and wider on the left side of the brain than on the right. This has very important implications, because this is the area for speech reception.

Actually, the precise area of the brain that has been found to be asymmetrical is the planum temporale, which is in the temporal lobe (the lower lateral lobe of either hemisphere) of the brain. This area of the brain has come under intense scrutiny by researchers and psychologists since the 1990s because they have found it to be involved in developmental dyslexia. Dyslexics tend to have an equal-size planum on both sides of their brain, whereas nondyslexics have a longer and wider one on the left side.

The implications here are that having a different type

of dominance pattern may be deleterious to one's reading skills. The area for phonological skills (sound reception and interpretation), normally on the left side, might not be fully developed in these people. If that is the case, the right side might take over these skills, or they might be shared, in which case the brain may be forced to choose between the two sometimes conflicting images. Additionally there is some evidence that the right side of the brain does not perform these functions as well as the left. One possible consequence of this sort of compensation is letter reversals, such as substituting a *b* for a *d*. This is normal in many children between the ages of 4 and 7 years, when they are first learning to read and write. But if there is competition for a skill within the brain, there may be continued confusion.

Of course, this does not mean that all left-handers are at risk, because we do not know whether they tend to have equal planum on both sides of their brain. My favorite quotation regarding the relationship between left-handedness and dyslexia comes from Dr. Rita Rudel, who for many years worked as a neuropsychologist at Columbia–Presbyterian Medical Center. She observed, "Most dyslexics are right-handed, and most left-handers can read." We still don't know much more than that, because left-handers are so often excluded from studies of which they are not the sole focus. There are presently no firm statistics on the number of dyslexics who are left-handed, yet many people believe that the percentage of left-handedness is higher in dyslexics than in the normal population.

## Asymmetries

There are often slight differences in the size, shape, and position of eyes and ears. Smiles are often crooked and feet differ in size. Asymmetries are a standard component of all forms of life. Of course some differences are more pronounced than others, but whether we notice these asymmetries or not, they exist everywhere throughout nature. Plants, animals, rock formations, the stars, and the planets are all asymmetrical. Even cells viewed through a microscope are asymmetrical.

Most people develop some degree of lateral preference, or sidedness, not only for their hands but also for their feet, eyes, and ears. We know that right-handers tend to be more compartmentalized with respect to their brain functioning; that is, speech and language and other logical functions are always on the left side of the brain, whereas music and art, creative functions, and emotional expression are on the right side.

But for left-handers the situation is more complex; their dominance patterns may be quite different depending on the individual. Some left-handers have a lateralization pattern very similar to that of right-handers (language on left, creative on right), some have reversed dominance (language on right), and some have mixed patterns, with language on both sides. This is called bilateralization of language. What this means in practical terms is that they have different aspects of language on each side of their brains. In cases where these people suffer an injury to one side of the brain, such as in a stroke, the other side can more easily take over all language functions.

Beyond that, no one knows what the benefits and risks are of having different types of lateralization patterns. Some researchers view any deviation from the "normal" dominance pattern as being problematic, but others disagree. I believe each individual needs to be assessed with an open mind. And most importantly, if someone is not experiencing difficulties, there is probably no cause for concern.

## What Does It Mean to Be Left-Handed?

The whole area of assessment of hand preference is complicated, as discussed in Chapter Three. To most people, being left-handed means writing with the left hand. To specialists in the field, it can mean a variety of things, but most researchers accept the writing hand as a basic way to distinguish groups of children and adults. Of course this approach is valid only in countries where hand preference for writing is not switched (the United States, Canada, and most of Europe). In countries where left-handers are switched for writing, one has to look at other indicators, like the throwing hand or the hand used for brushing teeth, combing hair, sewing, using tools, participating in sports, and so on. This is often difficult, which is why we have long yet imperfect (as discussed earlier) questionnaires that ask a myriad of questions about hand preference.

Most adults tend to think of themselves as either right-handed or left-handed depending on which hand they write with or which hand generally performs a

Most specialists accept the writing hand as an indication of overall handedness, and most people identify their handedness according to what hand they write with.

particular set of tasks. In fact, by the age of 6 years, most children have found a clear preference. The purpose of tests and questionnaires is not to cast doubt on those who are confident and know their own preferences. The tests exist to help us gain a clearer understanding of how the brain works and of the causes and consequences of the entire range of lateral preferences. For your purposes, all that really matters is your self-knowledge and your understanding of those around you.

## What Does It Mean to Be Ambidextrous?

Ambidextrous people can use either hand equally well for both fine and gross motor tasks, even difficult practiced tasks like writing and drawing. This is why very few people qualify for this designation (only about 1 percent of the population). Although in theory being ambidextrous should be less difficult for someone lacking the right-shift factor, there is no evidence that one can learn to be ambidextrous. However, many individuals can learn to use their nonpreferred hand when their dominant hand is injured.

Only about 1 percent of the population can be considered truly ambidextrous, which is having the ability to do all activities equally well with both hands.

## Are Lefties Brain Damaged?

Some lefties have indeed suffered injury to their brains. When this occurs, the resultant condition is known as pathological left-handedness, a term coined by neuropsychologist Dr. Paul Satz to differentiate between this group and genetically natural left-handers. This term sounds dire, but all it means is that the child is left-handed because of some pathology that occurred in his or her brain early in life.

Any number of things can happen in utero, prenatally (before birth), or perinatally (around the time of birth) to cause brain dysfunction. The two most obvious examples are hemorrhage (literally a small stroke) or anoxia (a deficiency of oxygen), which is the most common form of damage that occurs at this time in development.

When the damage occurs, whatever its causes, it often occurs in the motor fibers descending from the motor strip of the cerebral cortex—this system is called the pyramidal system (because it resembles a pyramid)—and it courses from the cerebral cortex all the way to the spinal cord. As mentioned earlier, there are numerous potential consequences of this sort of injury.

The fibers descending from the left cerebral cortex affect the motor movement of the right side of the body (lower part of arm, all of the hand and fingers, and lower part of leg, and some of the eye muscles and tongue). Therefore, if the damage occurs on the left side of the brain the child may have a weaker right side. If the damage is severe enough, then the child can be spastic (cerebral palsy) or hemiplegic (paralyzed) on the right side of his or her body. When this happens, the brain compensates by shifting language and motor dominance over to the right side of the brain. Consequently, even though nature probably did not intend it, this child will become a lefty.

Sometimes these children have learning difficulties, but often they do not. When they do have developmental problems, many people attribute this to their left-handedness. But their left-handedness has nothing to do with their learning problems. The early brain injury is the culprit in both the left-handedness and the learning difficulties.

When this same type of damage occurs on the right side of the brain, the left side of the body will be affected, and the child will be right-handed, so there is such a thing as pathological right-handedness. These children can also be spastic or hemiplegic. However, unless they display symptoms of these conditions, we might not as readily notice them because they are using the hand that everyone else does, and it's likely they would have been right-handed anyway.

I see many "pathological" left-handers in my practice. They often cannot use their right arm and hand, and they may have learning difficulties. But there is nothing pathological about them. They are smart, sweet, creative, funny, and interesting kids. I've been following one of these children, whom I'll call Dana, for many years. Dana identifies with left-handers and doesn't view herself as different from others. She is fairly well coordinated, bright, and resourceful. Most important, she has a lot of courage and perseverance. I know that Dana will be very successful in life.

## From the Beginning: Preferences in the Womb

There is evidence that the uterine environment can influence lateralization. We know from Dr. Norman Geschwind's theories that an excess of testosterone in utero may play a role in brain development and in the development of laterality. Because the fetal bond between a mother and baby is biologically and psychologically so strong, there is a slightly higher correlation between the child's handedness and the mother's handedness than between the child's handedness and the father's handedness.

## Theories and Testing

Brain–behavior relationships in children are very complex and difficult to study because the young brain is constantly changing. The system is not static; therefore, we are forced to make inferences without being absolutely certain. We used to believe that cerebral dominance developed very slowly in children, that they didn't actually develop laterality until the age of 12 or 13. This belief was based, in part, on observations of children who were born with brain tumors or who suffered severe seizures. In the most serious cases, doctors would actually remove the affected hemisphere. What they then found was that as the children grew older, the remaining hemisphere would tend to take over the functions normally associated with the absent side.

We now know that if a child loses one side of his or her brain very early in life, he or she will show remarkable recovery, but some skills will be less than perfect. On the other hand, if an injury to one side of the brain is sustained after the age of 2 years, the child will have developmental delays that mimic what we see in adult victims of stroke—speech or language delay if the left side is damaged, and problems with spatial perception, emotional expression, and so forth if the right side is damaged. This is how we know that the brain of a 2-year-old is already lateralized for these skills. Also, the recent studies of infants show ear preferences for speech and sounds.

There are even signs of laterality in utero. We have reason to believe you inherit a propensity for dominance from your parents and that it is present at or prior to birth. Of course these preferences are very plastic in young children, but they are present nonetheless. For the most part, excluding injuries or illness, children act in the way they are genetically ordained to act. However, environment can play a role, particularly for those who do not have a right-shift gene. The fact that twins, who are, in theory, genetically identical, don't always share laterality suggests that there are indeed other elements involved.

The conclusions of different studies are often divergent. No matter what theory of laterality you consider, there are characteristics and examples that seem to disprove it. Where one theory might account for some of the observed facts, another will account for others. But there still is no single theory that can account for all the disparate findings.

Assessment is another confusing subject. Of course, most adults correctly refer to themselves as left-handed, right-handed, or ambidextrous. They know what they need to know and they don't need to answer a series of questions to make it clear to them. There have been and continue to be studies involving adults, but these are performed to teach researchers and physicians more about lateralization and the human brain.

For children, the issue of testing is more complex and more critical. If by the age of 6 years a child is still uncertain of his or her lateral preferences, particularly for writing, it can cause confusion and make it difficult to develop proficiency. By testing a child, we can begin

---

Many children prefer to use their left hands for fine motor skills, such as writing and brushing their teeth, and their right hands for larger motor skills, such as throwing or batting a baseball.

to understand where his or her preferences lie and which side may be more proficient for certain skills.

We would do this in conjunction with other sensori-motor, perceptual, and language tasks to ensure that the confusion the child is experiencing is not due to other developmental problems. Once we understand the strengths and weaknesses of the child and what his or her natural preferences are, we can begin to develop proficiency in the language, perceptual, and motor skills the child needs to succeed in first grade.

This does not mean that a child must perform all skilled tasks with the same hand. Some children prefer to use their left hands for fine motor skills such as writing and brushing their teeth and their right hands for skills such as throwing or batting a baseball. In fact, about half of all left-handers have mixed preferences. Even many right-handed children have mixed preferences. As long as the child consistently uses the same hand for a given activity, such as writing, this is not a problem.

The more a child uses a particular hand for a given task, the more proficient he or she will become. However, if, for instance, the child switches back and forth between hands for writing, the brain circuits that would normally develop may get confused and he or she will have difficulty developing proficiency.

If a child still seems uncertain of hand preferences through kindergarten, it may be a good idea to do an assessment of specific motor skills to see which side he or she prefers and which side is more proficient. Sometimes a child will prefer to use his or her left hand for writing but will not know how to get started or will be confused by watching right-handers. I have been called in on a number of cases such as this, and I generally find it fairly easy to determine the child's natural preferences.

I don't use the handedness questionnaire I developed with Dr. Geschwind, because it's strictly for adults. It was also designed for research and not for clinical purposes. Shorter questionnaires are used clinically. A neuromotor exam for children was developed by Dr. Martha Denckla, a pediatric neurologist with whom I worked at Columbia–Presbyterian in 1979 and 1980 (she was Dr. Rita Rudel's colleague). We wrote a paper together about our study of motor coordination in 100 left-handed children. That exam included a lateral preference questionnaire for children that I still use in conjunction with sensorimotor, perceptual, and language tasks. It consists of the following items:

Say to the child, "Show me how you . . ." then circle *L, R,* or both *L* and *R* next to each item.

| | |
|---|---|
| Look through a hole in paper | L / R |
| Kick a ball | L / R |
| Step on a bug | L / R |
| Write | L / R |
| Comb hair | L / R |
| Brush teeth | L / R |
| Cut with scissors | L / R |
| Throw a ball | L / R |
| Hit ball with a bat | L / R |

| | |
|---|---|
| Use a racket | L / R |
| Hammer a nail | L / R |
| Use a screwdriver | L / R |
| Cut food with a knife | L / R |
| Flip a coin | L / R |
| Open door with a key | L / R |

Parents and teachers need to realize that some of these items are more useful than others; for example, screwdrivers and keys are often designed to be used with the right hand. It's difficult to design the perfect handedness questionnaire for children, but we try! By the way, the results of our motor coordination study indicated that left-handers develop motor coordination similar to right-handers.

## Changing from Lefty to Righty— Advantage or Abuse?

In spite of the difficulties left-handers sometimes face, there is no advantage to attempting to switch your child's lateral preferences. In fact, there may be significant disadvantages.

I have spoken to a great many children, adolescents, and adults who believe or know for certain that their handedness was switched. They feel deprived and resentful. Many of them feel as though something important and unique has been taken away from them, and they wonder about the possible deleterious effects of this on their brain and their personality. I tell them what I know, and I also tell them that if they were very clumsy and uncoordinated before their handedness was switched, then it is quite likely that they would have been clumsy regardless of whether they were using their right hand or their left hand. This is because clumsiness is not caused by the hand you use but rather by the brain areas that are responsible for coordination and motor control. Of course, switching handedness probably does not improve the situation at all—and may make it worse, because the brain has to lay down new connections.

The fact is that handedness is a consequence of what is occurring in the brain and does not cause changes in the brain. Contrary to what some experts have suggested, switching handedness does not help to organize the brain. Children are born with a certain brain organization, and trying to switch their handedness is only going to cause confusion. The confusion caused by switching a child's handedness can lead to problems such as difficulties distinguishing left from right, frustration, and possibly stammering and stuttering.

---

In spite of the difficulties left-handers may face, there is no advantage to switching your child's lateral preferences. In fact, there may be disadvantages, including difficulty distinguishing left from right and even stuttering and stammering.

## Conclusion

The fact is that a certain portion of the population has always been left-handed. This has been confirmed by cave drawings and by investigating the damage done to ancient skulls by a mix of left- and right-handed hunters and assailants seemingly similar to present-day numbers.

As you can see, the majority of the scientific discussion regarding lateral preferences is focused on genetics, brain organization, and the role proficiency plays in determining handedness. Although this is all interesting to me as a scientist, and hopefully to you, our overriding concern is making the most of nature's choices. I think it is important to have an understanding of the elements that form us, of how we got where we are. But whatever the causes of lateralization, it is the consequences to you and your children and how to best address them that ultimately motivated me to write this book.

### Famous Lefty Actors

- Dan Aykroyd
- Tim Allen
- Jason Alexander
- Kim Basinger
- Bruce Boxleitner
- Matthew Broderick
- Carol Burnett
- George Burns
- James Caan
- Jim Carrey

- Charlie Chaplin
- Tom Cruise
- Olivia de Havilland
- Robert DeNiro
- Matt Dillon
- Fran Drescher
- Richard Dreyfuss
- Peter Fonda
- Morgan Freeman
- Greta Garbo
- Terri Garr
- Whoopie Goldberg
- Cary Grant
- Mark Hamill
- Rex Harrison
- Goldie Hawn
- Jim Henson
- Rock Hudson
- Diane Keaton
- Nicole Kidman
- Val Kilmer
- Lisa Kudrow
- Michael Landon
- Spike Lee
- Ray Liotta
- Shirley MacLaine
- Howie Mandel
- Julianna Margulies
- Harpo Marx
- Mary Stuart Masterson
- Marlee Matlin

- Andrew McCarthy
- Steve McQueen
- Marilyn Monroe
- Rick Moranis
- Ryan O'Neal
- Sarah Jessica Parker
- Anthony Perkins
- Ron Perlman
- Luke Perry
- Joe Piscopo
- Richard Pryor
- Robert Redford
- Keanu Reeves
- Julia Roberts
- Ginger Rogers
- Eva Marie Saint
- Telly Savalas
- Jerry Seinfeld
- Christian Slater
- Rod Steiger
- Emma Thompson
- Dick Van Dyke
- Bruce Willis
- Oprah Winfrey
- Mare Winningham
- James Woods
- Joanne Woodward

# Chapter
## Five

# *Helping Your Lefty with the Basics—Physically and Emotionally*

As I demonstrated in Chapter One, many of the tasks and activities that right-handers take for granted, like winding a wristwatch or trying to cut with right-handed scissors, may present the left-handed child with difficulty and even danger. In certain areas, such as writing, these difficulties can be apparent from the child's earliest efforts. But there are dozens of less obvious frustrations. Often, what uninformed right-handed parents view as clumsiness or immaturity in their left-handed child may be a result of these challenges and frustrations.

There are also children who, for one reason or another, have specific learning disabilities. Although some researchers may argue otherwise, there is no compelling scientific reason to believe that learning disabilities are more common in left-handed children. They can affect any child, regardless of his or her lateral preferences. Recognizing and addressing your child's problems now could enable you to minimize their negative impact in the future.

## Recognizing and Understanding Learning Challenges

Neuroscientists and neuropsychologists now believe that the majority of learning differences and disabilities are related to differences in the brain's structure and circuitry. Because all brains develop differently, the areas that may be suited to a particular task in one brain may not be as well suited to that same task in another. Some of this differentiation is the result of prenatal or perinatal trauma and some of it is inherited. A child whose parents are both musicians is likely to display a greater degree of natural musical facility than is the child of two accountants. If a child's parents are especially verbal or athletic, he or she may have a genetic inclination toward related skills. None of this is guaranteed, however. Accountants can produce talented musicians and artists, and athletes can produce nuclear physicists. There is still some mystery involved in how we become who and what we are. Regardless of genetics and brain circuitry, any child can be stimulated and virtually any skill can be improved on. Early exposure and focused stimulation both play a significant role in how each child develops.

Your first step should be to try to determine your child's strengths and weaknesses so that you can encourage the strengths and assist him or her in those areas that present a challenge. That's essentially what I do in my practice. I work closely with each child and attempt to establish which skills he or she is good at and which ones need improvement. Then, using my knowledge of the human brain as a model, I correlate the child's skills and deficiencies with the areas of the brain that are responsible for those functions. When I have a sense of how the child is functioning and what the challenges are, I'm able to make assumptions and inferences about his or her brain circuitry and how things are developing. Only when I have a clear understanding of each individual do I make a statement to the parents describing what seems to be developing properly and what is not working quite as well.

On the basis of the child's age (preschool versus school age) and whether a particular problem is mild, moderate, or severe, I make my recommendations concerning how to address it. In younger children, mild problems do not necessarily require outside intervention. I generally have the parents work with the child at home to increase exposure and stimulation in the areas where the child appears to be falling behind. For instance, I might give them fine motor coordination exercises to perform with their children, such as making vertical and horizontal lines and drawing shapes and patterns. In some cases the children will be asked to verbally describe what they are drawing as they draw it to help strengthen the connection between movement and speech. These are not tests but exercises that can help to lay a foundation for printing, cursive writing, and other motor and verbal skills. Kinesthetic writing programs such as Rhythmic Writing, and Loops and Other Groups, which can be ordered through Therapy Skill Builders—(800) 872-1726—serve this purpose quite well.

Often, in these milder cases, I will suggest that a teacher also become involved in this focused stimulation, particularly with preschool and kindergarten children. Of course, parents can advocate for their own children if they see a problem such as the ones I describe here. This is easier if you get acquainted with and develop a positive relationship with your child's teachers from the beginning of the school year. Preschool teachers tend to have more time and flexibility than elementary school teachers do. Consequently, they are able to pay special attention to those children who require it. This approach is often all that is required to achieve a turnaround for children with mild problems. Of course, if a child is older, even a mild problem can prevent him from learning optimally in the classroom. In this case, I would follow the recommendations below.

If my testing shows that a child has a moderate problem, in addition to making specific suggestions to the parents and teacher and constructing a customized program of exercises, I will most likely recommend an outside consultant to work with the child. Depending on the nature of the problem, I will suggest one of three professionals:

- **A speech therapist:** a person who specializes in the treatment of speech defects and disorders through the use of exercises and audiovisual aides
- **A learning specialist:** someone who works with people who have learning disabilities rooted in brain function
- **An occupational therapist:** an individual who treats and rehabilitates people with motor skill problems and other physical disabilities

I've also used a combination of these professionals when necessary. In addition, I continue to monitor the child's progress myself. If not properly addressed early on, a moderate problem will almost undoubtedly become more severe in time. Remember speech and movement form the foundation for everything a child does in school. Children need these skills to keep up with their classmates, to feel good about themselves, and to progress in their learning and development.

Unfortunately, severe problems often require more serious measures. The first step is a very comprehensive evaluation, which should include medical, psychological, learning, speech, and sensorimotor components. This would usually be followed by enrollment in a special program with a small group of children who face similar challenges. In general, these programs will involve speech therapists and occupational therapists who work closely with the children to help build those skills that are lagging. Early intervention programs provide the best start for children with multiple learning disabilities and handicaps.

## Parental and Teacher Assessment

From the time a child is about 2 years old and on through elementary school, middle school, and even into high school, he or she will give numerous signals that can alert parents and teachers of a problem.

For example, parents may notice that a child is struggling with speech, having trouble choosing the proper words to express a thought, or finding it difficult to pronounce certain words. One child may have difficulty retelling stories; another might appear to be having problems with his or her balance. Any one of these scenarios may indicate a problem.

Comparing your child with playmates of a similar age is a good way to establish whether the child is progressing appropriately for his or her age. If you notice that these other children are more articulate or seem better coordinated than your child, it is probably wise to keep your eye on these areas of development. Your pediatrician might also help to define what your expectations should be. Of course all children develop differently, and differences don't necessarily signal problems. But if your child appears to be lagging behind in a particular skill or activity, continue to watch that area. If the perceived problem persists and you feel that you should take action, you may want to discuss it with the child's teachers.

Because teachers have a very different perspective from that of parents, their input can be extremely valuable. Although many parents are active and eager participants in their children's education at home, they may not know how much exposure their child has had to a particular area of learning in the school environment. For example, many preschool teachers do not formally teach preacademic skills such as the alphabet or writing letters, whereas others do. Some 4-year-olds may be learning how to hold a pencil or crayon properly to draw and write, whereas others may not be exposed to this skill in school until they are 5 years old. Barbara Gabriele, the head teacher of the threes class at the Infant Toddler Development Center in Ridgewood, New Jersey, teaches her children (who will all have turned 4 by the following September) a variety of fine motor skills such as cutting with scissors and holding a pencil. She uses grips or other aids to help the children hold their writing implements in a comfortable way so that they have good control. However, she does not teach them how to write; that skill they learn later. If she sees that a child is having particular problems with fine motor skills, though, she tends not to worry about this too much unless there are other problems as well.

Because teachers are able to watch children interact with one another and can compare the progress of any individual with a sizable group, they are often the first outsiders to notice developmental problems. Consequently, they are sometimes the first to bring them to the attention of the parents. Of course, most parents already have an inkling that something is not quite right, and they are often relieved when someone else notices it too.

Additionally, children tend to behave differently in different environments. If, after careful observation, your child's teacher feels a problem is serious enough, he or she may recommend an evaluation by a speech pathologist, psychologist, occupational therapist, or even a child neuropsychologist such as me who specializes in working with children with learning problems.

As valuable as the observations made by a child's teachers and parents are, it's extremely important to bear in mind that all children grow and develop at different rates. Furthermore, minor problems will often work themselves out in a classroom setting. Once competition begins, it seems that children begin to work a little harder in order to keep up with their peers. But if you and your child's teachers ultimately conclude that a problem does exist, or even if you remain concerned about the possibility, having a professional evaluation by a child specialist can do no harm. If there's nothing wrong, you will be able to relax and continue to enjoy watching your child's growth, and if there is indeed a problem, you can begin to address it immediately.

## Physical Basics

### Eating

Before children learn to use eating utensils, when they are still grabbing at everything in sight with their busy little hands, all you need to do is place food in the center of their reach and let them pick it up with whichever hand they prefer to use. More often than not, they are likely to use both, or they may switch back and forth without any apparent cause or pattern. But once they begin to use forks and spoons, you may find yourself attempting to push them one way or another.

Although there are many different cultural biases regarding proper dining etiquette, the single most important consideration for your child is his or her comfort. If it is easier for your lefty to eat European style (the fork remains in one hand rather than switching back and forth for the tasks of cutting and eating) than to switch the fork back and forth, as has become the custom in the United States, there is no reason to fight against it. When a preference finally does begin to emerge, whatever it happens to be, your child must be allowed to go with his or her instincts and to develop proficiency. This way there will be fewer accidents and far less frustration.

## Drawing

When children first begin working with writing and drawing implements, they generally use crayons and markers on a large easel or paper. They often don't pick a preferred hand until they begin to develop some degree of proficiency. Until this occurs, you should simply allow them to work in a space where they can move around to find the position that works best for them.

Also, when you set up a play area, place the utensils and the paper or blackboard in the center of the child's body, so he or she can reach for them and use them with either hand. Make certain you have a variety of implements for your child to write and draw with and lots of different types of paper to use. This way your child will be more likely to remain interested and will continue to develop as he or she should.

## Reading

Numerous studies involving children with reading problems have been performed over the years. Since the early 1950s, when famous neurologist Dr. Samuel Orton first postulated that such problems might have something to do with left-brain/right-brain issues, this has been an area of great interest to neurologists, neuropsychologists, and learning disabilities specialists. The children Dr. Orton worked with, who were otherwise bright and competent, appeared to have childhood versions of stroke-related adult conditions, such as alexia (the sudden loss of the ability to read) and aphasia (the loss of the ability to articulate ideas or comprehend language). Dr. Orton noticed that a large percentage of the children in his population were left-handers. This and other such observations are what led to the belief that certain kinds of reading problems might be related to left-handedness. But because these studies were all done in clinical settings rather than with normal test samples, we have no way of determining if these children were genetic lefties or pathological lefties, that latter of whom would most likely have been in the clinics because of injuries suffered in utero.

In fact, when the late Dr. Philip Bryden, a highly respected Canadian neuropsychologist and laterality expert who was celebrated in the scientific community for his rigorous scientific methodology, took a team of researchers into the public schools to test theories of whether left- or mixed-handedness is related to reading problems, he was unable to find any relationship whatsoever. Because of time constraints, these researchers weren't able to do the kind of in-depth testing one can do in a clinical setting, but their research with large groups of children offered a convincing contradiction to earlier theories. We do know, however, that observations made in clinical settings are unlikely to be indicative of the normal population.

Although it is probably true that special clinics see more lefties than righties, this may simply be because their handwriting is messy, or they might stand out in other ways. Remember too that approximately three quarters of the children in these clinics are boys. And yet we know that boys do not account for 90 percent of learning disabilities. In fact, it is because boys tend to be louder and more active than their female counterparts that teachers and caretakers are more likely to notice it when a boy has a problem. Because of this, it may be wise to be even more attuned to the signals if you're raising a daughter. A similar model may well explain why we see a somewhat larger percentage of left-handers in these clinics. Simply put, left-handed children tend to stand out. If they are writing differently or making reversals when they write (which many left-handers do when they are learning to write), teachers may think they are dyslexic. Yet this situation may be a good thing, for if a problem is not noticed in the classroom or at home, it may not be addressed.

## Writing

Most of the advice that applies to drawing can also be applied to the earliest efforts to write. Always give your child a large space in which to work, place writing instruments where he or she can easily reach them with either hand, and allow enough time to develop proficiency before you concern yourself with which hand your child prefers.

Remember that only when a child has developed some proficiency should you expect him or her to choose one hand with which to work. Even then, there may be some switching back and forth if the preferred hand becomes tired or cramped, but in time a clear preference should begin to emerge. Of course, if you are raising a lefty, there are some specific issues you should be aware of.

Use a large chalkboard when teaching a lefty to write. This enables the child to use the larger muscles in his arm as well as his fingers. Place your own left hand over the child's to guide his movements.

## Why Lefties Tilt Their Notebooks and Hook Their Hands

About 50 percent of left-handers hook their hands when they write. More than half of them are boys. Many left-handers prefer to print, and for some reason they don't tend to hook as much when printing as when writing in script. We believe this is because writing in script requires finer motor skills.

For years we assumed that left-handed children hooked their hands to enable them to view what they are writing. But because some right-handers hook their hands and because there are left-handers who hook in Israel and other cultures where they write from right to left, this theory doesn't appear to stand up.

Dr. Jerre Levy, a very well-respected neuropsychologist, posited the theory of why some left-handers hook when they write that seems to make the most sense. She theorized that lefties who hook have language located on the left side of their brains and that the lefties who don't hook have language located in the right side of their brains. If language is located on the left side of the brain, as it is in about 80 percent of the population and at least 60 percent of the left-handed population, and if the writing center is on the right side, as it is for most lefties, the language information has to cross the corpus callosum to get to the motor area on the right side. The brain actually has to construct a path for this information to travel from one side of the brain to the other.

Though still controversial, there is a theory that when

Lefties often find it easier to write curvy letters than to print, even though cursive seems to go "the wrong way" for them. They should be taught the modified cursive form, also known as the DeNealian alphabet, which is a cross between print and script.

information has to cross the corpus callosum to get from one side of the brain to the other, the information appears as a mirror image. According to this theory, a person who hooks his or her hand must do so to reverse the information a second time, to make it come out as it went in. They write backwards and almost upside down to get the information to come out properly. It may be that those right-handers who hook, many of whom come from left-handed families, have language located on the right side of their brains.

Whatever the causes, if it turns out that your child is among those who need to hook their hand to write legibly, and he or she is comfortable, there is no reason to discourage it. It may be the only way he or she can contend with the mysteries of the brain.

## Mirror Script

Letter reversals are very common through kindergarten and even into first grade for both right- and left-handed children. Left-handers may reverse letters more often than right-handers when they are first learning to write. This is because the left hand turns in the opposite direction from the right hand. And, if Dr. Levy's theory regarding hooked writing is correct, it could also offer a credible explanation for mirror script. Children who write in reverse may simply be writing the words as they see them. But if the behavior continues after first grade, it might be time to take steps to address it.

Before taking any drastic measures, you should sit down with your child and practice writing skills. Use a large pad with wide spaces between the lines and make certain the child is comfortable. If the situation doesn't improve in time, you may want to consider an evaluation to determine the causes and decide on the best approach for remediation. Under most circumstances, this will involve special exercises and some time with a tutor or an occupational therapist.

## A Case History

A few years ago, I treated a 5-year-old boy I'll call Josh. In addition to an early injury to two fingers on his right hand, Josh had graphomotor (fine motor skills—especially writing) problems related to early brain damage caused by trauma at birth. He seemed to be having trouble developing handedness when he was in kindergarten. When the teacher informed the parents that Josh was constantly switching back and forth in class, they couldn't understand what was wrong, because he always wrote with his left hand at home. When Josh came to see me for a consultation, I set him up at a desk and let him work with some drawing and printing. He used his right hand for everything he did, and when I asked him if he was sure he wanted to use that hand he assured me that he did. He calmly informed me that he always used that hand.

We chatted for a while, and, before he left, I mentioned to him that I am left-handed and I showed him how I write. When he came in the following week, I decided to have him perform some of the same motor tasks we'd done the week before. I fully expected him to use his right hand, but he surprised me; he used his left hand for everything he did. When I asked him why he was writing with his left hand now, he told me it was more comfortable for him.

Apparently, when he realized I was left-handed, he decided it would be okay to do what was most natural. Despite the fact that his parents were both right-handed, he was not uncomfortable at home. But in school, where he felt he had to conform, he felt compelled to write the same way the teacher and most of the other students did. I spoke with the child's teacher, who agreed to make it clear to Josh that it was perfectly okay to write with his left hand in school. With the support of his parents and teacher and after working with me for about 4 months, Josh became comfortable and increasingly competent writing with his left hand. He even learned how to use a baseball bat with his left hand, a skill that he was particularly proud of.

While I was working with Josh, I noticed that he was able to calculate baseball statistics in his head. I alerted his parents, and they gave me permission to give him some math tests. As it turned out, he was remarkably mathematically precocious. I told the parents about a special program for mathematically precocious children at Johns Hopkins University, and Josh eventually entered that program. Had he been left to struggle with his handedness, this very talented child would have been terribly frustrated and might have developed other problems. Without the teacher's consciousness of the difficulty, and without the attention he subsequently received, he might not have had the opportunity to develop or demonstrate his skills in math. Today, this young man is doing extremely well and is perfectly comfortable as a lefty.

Chances are that your left-handed child will have no more difficulty with most skills than any normal right-handed child will. But with any child, the possibility exists that a problem will emerge. See Chapter Nine for a comprehensive list of signs that might indicate whether your child has a learning problem.

## Emotional Basics

### Positive Reinforcement—Advantages of Being a Lefty

Some children are shorter than others; some are a little thinner. Some children have difficulty pronouncing certain consonants, and others have freckles and red hair. Whatever it is that sets your child apart, it is important to give him or her a sense of pride, a feeling that whatever it is that makes him or her special is a good thing.

In this way, left-handed children are no different from others. Very often they don't understand why they are doing things differently from those around them. It is up to you to explain what this means and to put it in a positive light.

A good way to begin is by helping them to develop an initial interest in left-handedness. This should not be a difficult task. Children are eager learners, and the fact is that lefties are well represented in many significant fields. Tell your lefty about the many famous left-handers in sports, music, entertainment, science, politics, and the fine arts—you'll find lists of them at the end of most chapters of this book. If you offer your support and guidance, your child will learn to think of him- or herself as special and begin to feel the sense of pride all children should enjoy.

## Tips and Techniques for Encouragement

Whether it is a hearing issue, a problem with vision, or difficulty working at a school desk, children often have special needs. These children might very well require a little extra support and guidance, but that is by no means the only thing they require. It is equally crucial that they are taught when, how, and whom to ask for help. Children need to understand that it's okay to ask their teachers and caretakers for a different desk, for a

---

Buy some basic tools especially for left-handers, such as scissors, rulers, watches, and even baseball mitts, if your left-handers like to play baseball.

---

better position in the classroom, or for the tools they need to feel comfortable at home or in school.

Make it clear that it is perfectly fine to use a different hand from the one you use for a given task. Help your child understand that it's okay to write differently and to perform some tasks with the right hand if that is more comfortable. Most important, help your child learn to trust his or her instincts.

If your lefty happens to be clumsy or uncoordinated, there may be no connection whatsoever between the clumsiness and the left-handedness. I know quite a few clumsy right-handers, but no one concludes that there is a relationship between their handedness and their clumsiness. Always focus on your child's special talents rather than the difficulties he or she is experiencing.

Finally, don't underestimate the importance of appropriate tools and equipment. A relatively small investment in left-handed pens, pencils, grips, rulers, notebooks, and desks can make a substantial difference to your lefty.

### Tips for Frustrated Right-Handed Parents— Teaching Your Lefty

Many right-handed parents assume their lefty will learn skills the same way they did. But all children are not identical. They may be equal, but they are very different from one another. And left-handers are inherently different from right-handers—not better or worse—but certainly different. The fact is that a left-handed child who observes a right-handed parent or teacher may be seeing

Face your child when teaching skills and simple tasks like tying shoes or using a fork. This way, he or she can mirror you easily.

some things in reverse. Additionally, left-handers' brains sometimes function differently from their right-handed counterparts.

If a right-handed parent tries to teach a left-handed child to write by placing his or her right hand over the child's left, it may take extra time, or it may not work at all. Most likely, unless you are very patient, it will cause frustration for both the parent and child. Remember that your child is an individual and that your lefty is different.

Simple adjustments in your behavior can make life much easier, much less frustrating for both of you. One useful technique is to have a left-handed family member or friend teach your lefty tasks such as writing and tying shoes.

I'm left-handed, but my daughter is predominantly right-handed. It made more sense for me to have my right-handed husband teach her some of the fine motor skills I might have helped her with if we shared lateral preferences. If a left-hander is not readily available, you can try to teach your child by using your left hand, or in the case of tasks such as shoe tying, try sitting across from your child and having him or her mirror your movements. Children are excellent and eager observers.

They love to learn, and if you give them the proper model they will generally learn quickly.

There is also the issue of shirt and blouse sleeves getting stained by lead, crayons, ink, and markers. Of course, if children are able to roll up their sleeves, this will become less of a problem, but when your arm follows your writing implement across page after page, you're going to pick up some of whatever you're writing with. As parents, we have to do our best to contain our frustration regarding those issues we cannot control.

For some reason, what seems to cause the greatest confusion in parents is when a child chooses to perform certain tasks with the left hand and others with the right. For instance, many parents who aren't at all troubled by the fact that a child holds a pencil with his or her left hand seem to become distressed and concerned when that same child demonstrates a preference for the right hand when cutting food or tossing a ball.

The fact is that although most right-handers are strictly right-handed for most tasks, left-handers are far more likely to be mixed-handed. Although it may confuse some parents, this behavior is perfectly natural and should not be discouraged. In some ways this sort of flexibility can be viewed as a gift—more on this in Chapter Ten.

The overarching message here is to allow your child to grow and develop as naturally as possible. Children are very malleable, and most of the development that needs to take place will take care of itself if you offer your support, guidance, and love.

## Famous Lefty Writers, Journalists, and Other Wordsmiths

- James Baldwin
- Dave Barry
- Peter Benchley
- Bet Bowen
- Lewis Carroll
- Richard Condon
- Jean Genet
- Caroline Kennedy (also lawyer)
- John F. Kennedy Jr. (also lawyer)
- Ted Koppel
- Marshall McLuhan
- Edward R. Murrow
- Dr. Diane Paul
- Helen Hooven Santmyer
- Forrest Sawyer
- Viktoria Stefanov
- Mark Twain
- H. G. Wells
- Jessamyn West
- Eudora Welty

**Chapter
Six**

## *Making Your Environment
Lefty Friendly*

In addition to your patient understanding and gentle
guidance, there are a great many active steps you can
take to help make your child's environment lefty
friendly. Whether organizing a closet, setting the dinner
table, or arranging furniture, careful planning can
increase your child's comfort. And with items such
as kitchen utensils and power tools, your efforts can
actually reduce the likelihood of accidents and injury.

### Conveniences for Your Lefty—Nonintrusive
### Changes to Family Rooms

Many families these days have common work areas—
desks or tables where various family members are able

to work at different times. To accommodate both left-handers and right-handers, these family desks or computer stations should be as spacious as your home allows. If the computer is situated near the center of the desk or table and there is ample space on either side, both lefties and righties can, with a few quick adjustments, make the work area comfortable for them. Each user can place reading materials, pencils, and other tools wherever he or she finds convenient.

One of the tools many people fail to consider when attempting to address the challenges left-handers face is the computer mouse. A great majority of these devices are ergonomically shaped for the right hand, and the button that gets the majority of use is conveniently positioned for right-handed users. Fortunately, we are no longer forced to live with this. Left-handed mice, which are now readily available (see Resources), can make pointing and clicking a little easier for lefties. For families who share a computer and need to switch back and forth between left-handers and right-handers, a trackball with a long enough cable to move it to either side of the computer is probably a more sensible idea. Most

---

Arrange a lefty-friendly workstation at home. Position the work light so that it shines over your lefty's right shoulder, and set up the computer with the mouse and pad to the left of the keyboard—or better yet, buy a computer with a centrally located trackball or fingerpad.

---

new keyboards have a mouse plug on either side to accommodate both left- and right-oriented mice.

Although you may not be aware of it, most newer computers have an option for a left-handed setup under "mouse options" in the control panel. This feature enables you to easily reverse the functions of the right and left clickers if you choose to use a standard mouse or trackball. If you have a laptop with a touchpad or pointing device, this may be the only alteration that's required when switching between righties and lefties. The simpler it is for your family to make these minor adjustments, the fewer problems you are likely to have.

Lightweight lamps that have long cords and can easily be repositioned can also make life in a multihanded household a little easier. Or, if you prefer, you might place one lamp on each side of the family workspace. Furthermore, if a floor or table lamp has a switch on the side and you are right-handed, you probably have the switch on the right side. A simple way to accommodate both camps is to turn the lamp so that the on/off switch or dimmer faces forward. Make sure you have left-handed rulers, pens, and pencils (non-smear utensils with left-handed grips) wherever the right-handed counterparts are stored. Other family members should be taught to accommodate any minor inconveniences without grumbling, so that your lefty isn't made to feel self-conscious about being different.

As important as your awareness and support are, you certainly don't need to obsess about every tiny detail of every room in your home. Some things may indeed present minor inconveniences, and there may be those issues that you miss, but children are very resilient, left-handed children more so than right-handed ones, because of their brains' inherent plasticity. As long as you address the major issues and those things that present dangers to health and safety, your left-handers will generally find their own solutions for the things you happen to overlook.

## Organizing Your Child's Room

Although there are no hard-and-fast rules regarding optimal furniture placement for left-handed children or adults, there are a number of steps you can take to reduce potential inconvenience and discomfort. Obviously, if your left-handed child has his or her own computer, it should be set up with a left-handed mouse placed on the left of the keyboard, or you should consider getting a computer with a centrally located trackball or fingerpad. You can also purchase left-handed keyboards, with the arrow and number keys on the left,

It might be beneficial for your lefty to learn how to use a "regular" computer keyboard, so that he can become comfortable with it—because this is what he or she will most likely encounter at school and eventually at work.

though many left-handed children might be perfectly comfortable using a standard keyboard.

Bedside tables and lamps should be placed with his or her convenience in mind, and switches should be easily accessible to his or her left hand. A left-handed modular desk, with the elbow rest and writing surface on the left side and the entry and storage space on the right, is a good option. It will reduce your child's discomfort and will probably increase his or her productivity.

If your child prefers entering and exiting the bed on a particular side, as some children do, take that into account when arranging the room. If there is one bedside table in the room, ask your child which side he or she would prefer to have it on, and always, with any child, allow for the possibility that you will have to move things around for a while. There is no blueprint for a left-hander's room, but if you allow your child to have some say as to how his or her room is arranged, you will be giving your child the opportunity to solve his or her own problems. In addition to instilling confidence and boosting self-esteem, problem solving is a crucial component of every child's intellectual development.

## Closet Organization

Although it isn't something most of us think about every day, the majority of right-handed people tend to organize their closets in roughly the same way: shirts, blouses, coats, and jackets facing the right-hand wall. The most obvious explanation for this is that with the clothing facing this way the right hand can easily undo buttons, snaps, and zippers to remove the garments from their hangers. To accommodate a left-handed child, you might simply try reversing this arrangement. With the hanger's hook facing away from you, face the garments to the left and hang them in the closet that way. It's also a good idea to let your child help you and to watch where he or she tends to place things. In addition to giving you a sense of what is comfortable for your child, this might be a good way to teach a child to keep his or her room organized and clean—a wonderful side benefit of including kids in this process!

## Your Kitchen: Proper Utensils and Equipment

Of course, toddlers are not likely to use your kitchen utensils, but when a child becomes old enough to work in the kitchen, you will need to be conscious of the tools that may present problems. For example, manual can openers are designed for right-handers and can be very difficult for a lefty to use without practice. Many knives, particularly specialty knives such as those for carving and cutting butter, are also designed for right-handed users. This is why it is especially important to teach your lefty how to use knives properly. Because there is little chance your child will be able to eliminate the need to use knives, he or she should know how to handle, hold, and cut with them. A good general cookbook like *The Joy of Cooking* will have basic rules for using knives. Take time to show your child these fundamentals as you teach him or her about other kitchen tools and rules. Frying pans and ladles may have a pour spout on only one side, making it more difficult for left-handers to pour out liquids, which are often dangerously hot. Buy ones that don't have a pour spout or that have spouts on both sides.

Again, the left-hander's brain is flexible, so these issues need not present serious problems, but it is important to be aware of possible dangers and difficulties so that you can avoid them. It's also extremely important for parents to keep in mind that what might appear to be a result of clumsiness may in fact be a battle with tools and utensils designed for the right-handed majority.

Additionally, as with eating, which I discussed in more detail in Chapter Five, safety and comfort should come before grace and local custom when your child is working with a fork and knife.

## Avoiding Potential Accidents

### Tools

Tools can present a serious danger to any child and should always be dealt with very cautiously. Never let your child use tools without careful training and supervision. Garden and power tools that are designed for right-handers can pose a great risk to left-handers. The most sensible thing you can do is to evaluate any tools and equipment very carefully before training your children to use them. And please don't let them use tools without your supervision until you are absolutely certain they're safe.

Listed below are some of the more potentially dangerous tools that I'm aware of:

- **Handsaws** and **circular saws**, almost without
  exception, are designed for right-handed use. Without proper training in their use, lefties can be at
  serious risk. If your child is interested in taking
  shop class, make sure the instructor knows that he
  or she will be dealing with a lefty so he or she can
  provide the right kind of training and make the
  proper accommodations.
- **Power drills** and **Dremel tools** often have important
  controls, such as lock-off switches, on the right.
  Additionally, some of them are designed to fit the
  user's right hand. Look for those that have controls
  located in the center top or bottom of the tool.

  Some power tools have fans designed to blow
  debris away from the user when held in the right
  hand. These same tools, when held in the left hand,
  may blow the debris toward the user. Eye protection
  is always a good idea, but it is absolutely critical
  when left-handers must use these tools.

  When buying any kind of power tool, go to a
  hardware or home supply store where tools are displayed so that you and your child can examine
  them, pick them up, and handle them. Never buy a
  tool on the basis of the picture on the box or at
  a store where you can't hold the tool or even try
  it out.
- **"Weed whackers"** can present a risk to the legs of
  left-handed users, and most **scythes**, **sickles**, and

Garden and power tools designed for right-handers can pose serious risk to lefties who don't know how to use them. Always supervise your child when he or she is first learning to use this type of equipment.

**pruners** are ergonomically designed for right-handed use. You can find garden tools that are not right-hand-oriented, however.

• **Sewing machines** can be awkward for some left-handed users. Again, if your child is interested in taking sewing classes, make sure the teacher knows he or she is left-handed. There's no reason why sewing can't be a hobby for a lefty.

Unfortunately, the above list may not be complete, so if you have any doubts about a particular tool, treat it with extra-special care.

### Sports Equipment

If your left-handed child is forced to struggle with hand-me-down right-handed baseball gloves, bowling balls, or golf clubs, he or she will be at a definite disadvantage. Of course, in sports such as tennis, football, and basketball, the equipment generally has no built-in bias, but in those sports where handedness comes into play, try to accommodate your child's needs as best you can. You'll find a more comprehensive discussion of sports and athletic equipment and instruction in Chapter Eight.

## Motor Vehicles

Automobiles in the United States are designed to be more comfortable for right-handed drivers. The ignition is on the right side, as are gearshifts, radio and heater controls, and most emergency brakes. Unfortunately, if a driver is left-handed, his or her dominant hand will be boxed in to some degree. But because young people are malleable, and because they won't have to unlearn driving on the left side of the car, there shouldn't be too much difficulty. Certainly, with time, patience, and proper training, left-handers can and do learn to drive as well and as safely as anyone else.

For many years now, Dr. Stanley Coren, an experimental psychologist at the University of British Columbia in Vancouver, has found that left-handed individuals may be more accident prone than their right-handed counterparts. Whether this is true is still unclear, as are the reasons if it is indeed true. To the best of my knowledge, state Departments of Motor Vehicles don't have the sort of statistics that would help us to corroborate or contradict this. Certainly the problem of right-handed power tools and automobiles could, as Coren claims, account for some difference between left- and right-handed accident rates. And in those left-handers who were not allowed as children to progress naturally, there could be an additional lack of confidence, which could undoubtedly lead to awkwardness. But the jury is still out regarding any clear connection to lateral preferences and inherent clumsiness.

Furthermore, as I stated earlier, because their brains tend to be more resilient than the brains of right-handers, left-handers will often adjust more easily, more quickly to any difficulties they encounter. In fact, we've known for many years that left-handed stroke victims often recover more quickly than their right-handed counterparts. Until recently, we didn't understand the reasons for this, but now we know that because left-handers' brain organization is much less rigid than that of right-handers, the unaffected side of the brain can more easily take over functioning from the affected side. This also explains why many left-handers can become comfortable using either hand to do certain tasks. Because there is no right-handed gene guiding their behavior, they are less locked in to one way of doing things. Their options are more open, and therefore adjustments to the environment are often less problematic for them than for right-handers.

## A Lefties World

Some researchers have argued that because left-handers' brains are more diffusely organized—not rigidly set up or compartmentalized like right-handers' brains—they may have different ways of thinking and different points of view. This suggests that left-handers may have an advantage when it comes to multimodal reasoning—the kind of reasoning that's required for advanced studies in areas such as science and psychology, just to name a few. This is only conjecture, however.

We don't know if this alters the child's point of view of his or her environment. However, I have known many left- and mixed-handed individuals who were extremely creative in how they set up their environments to suit their needs. I suspect that left-handers have always had the ability to be creative and to see things in different ways, so I am sure they can find many ways to organize their environments and even improve on existing structures.

This type of brain organization, and the flexibility that comes along with it, might help explain why I'm perfectly comfortable painting a wall either right- or left-handed. It could also explain why lefties often tend to demonstrate some level of ambidexterity in a wide variety of skills. My sense is that if you do what you can to make your environment more lefty friendly, your child will find creative ways to do the rest.

### Famous Lefty Musicians, Singers, and Composers

- Carl Philipp Emanuel Bach
- David Bowie
- David Byrne
- Glen Campbell
- Natalie Cole
- Phil Collins
- Billy Ray Cyrus
- Dick Dale
- Celine Dion
- Don Everly
- Phil Everly
- Bela Fleck
- Glenn Frey
- Eric Gales

- Judy Garland
- Erroll Garner
- Crystal Gayle
- Glenn Gould
- Kevin Griffin
- Isaac Hayes
- Thomas Hedley
- Jimi Hendrix
- Albert King
- Annie Lennox
- John Lydon (aka Johnny Rotten)
- Melissa Manchester
- Chuck Mangione
- Wynton Marsalis
- Paul McCartney
- George Michael
- Peter Nero
- Anthony Newley
- Robert Plant
- Cole Porter
- Sergei Rachmaninoff
- Lou Rawls
- Seal
- Paul Simon
- Ringo Starr
- Sting
- Rich Szabo
- Tiny Tim
- Rudy Vallee
- Lenny White
- Paul Williams

# Chapter
# Seven

## *School Daze: Making Sure Your Child's School Is Lefty Friendly and Lefty Positive*

Even without the additional issues that left-handedness can sometimes raise, the first year of school can be a very trying time for any child. This is the time when your child's horizons are broadened, the time when a new set of social skills begins to develop. It might well be the first time your son or daughter will be in someone else's care for an extended period of time, without the security of your calming presence. In addition to dealing with a whole new set of adults—the teachers and administrators—your child will be surrounded by a diverse group of peers. If things go well and your child learns to enjoy school, he or she will be far more likely to thrive than a child who dreads each new day. It is crucial that you do everything in your power to make the transition from life at home to the world outside a smooth one.

If your son or daughter is happy and comfortable in the school environment throughout kindergarten, you're off to a great start. But as crucial as the first year can be, there are numerous issues that might arise in the years that follow. These years are a critical time for the development of confidence, self-esteem, and learning skills. Fortunately, there is much you can do to help your child through all of the early school years and beyond.

## Talking with Your Lefty

The first step toward a successful transition should be to discuss with your child the issues he or she is likely to face in the new environment. Suggest techniques for responding to potential problems, without exaggerating these problems and creating unnecessary nervousness and stress. And remember not to focus solely on the difficulties; there is much about school that your child will look forward to and enjoy. Be sure to paint the overall picture as a fun and exciting one. Most important, make it clear to your child that it's okay to ask for help if he or she is uncomfortable or is struggling with supplies or equipment.

Another issue that deserves some attention is potential frustration and how to deal with it. One way to teach your child how to deal with frustration is by setting a good example at home. If you try to avoid angry outbursts when your child sees you becoming annoyed, he or she will follow your lead. This doesn't mean you should never become frustrated; what it means is that rather than displaying your temper without restraint, you should try to remain calm and look for solutions for the immediate problem. Remember, children learn very quickly to mirror the behavior of those around them. If possible, try to talk your son or daughter through the process of dealing with the problem that's causing the frustration. You may not always have the self-control to do this—most people don't. But you might find that by focusing on training your child how to properly deal with frustration, you are able to regain your own perspective.

You should also talk with your child about how to cope with any criticism that might arise. Use examples of the types of things people tend to criticize and offer logical, unemotional responses. Remind your child that differences are what make people distinct and special— these unique characteristics are often the very things that we recognize and love in one another. Use examples of what you love about your child or your spouse. Reinforce the idea that when people criticize others, it's often because they lack understanding, because they may not feel good about themselves, or because they feel the need to have someone to look down on. Make your child aware of how special he or she is to you and to your family. Remind him or her of the qualities and characteristics that you are proud of. Make certain your child knows that you are always ready and willing to help if a problem does develop and that it is always okay to come to you with any problems.

Left-handed children may have to work a little harder to write legibly; as a result, it might take them longer to complete tests and other assignments. Make sure that the teacher is aware of this so that he or she can build it into your child's schedule.

Handwriting is by far the most common and conspicuous problem that left-handed children have to tackle. Because of the awkward position these children's hands are sometimes forced into, and the fact that most of their teachers will be right-handed, the necessary skills might not come as quickly as they do for many of their right-handed classmates. Left-handed children may have to work a little harder to write legibly, and, consequently, it may take them a little longer to complete their tests and write papers. Children who understand why their classmates are finishing before them are far less likely to be frustrated by it than those who don't.

## A Few Basic Suggestions for Left-Handed Handwriting

Use a large surface like a blackboard when first teaching a child to write. This enables the child to use the larger muscles in his or her arms and fingers. Place your own left hand over the child's to guide his or her movements. Use a multisensory approach when teaching handwriting. For instance, engage the child's tactile sense by using letters and numbers that can be felt and manipulated (like raised lettering, plastic letters, etc.).

Engage the kinesthetic sense by having the child write with his or her eyes closed to focus on movements of the hand. Use verbal cues like *down* and *around* to describe motions of the hands. Lefties with handwriting and letter reversal problems often find it easier to write curvy letters than to print. But they may also have a hard time with learning strict cursive writing because the letters seem to be written "the wrong way" for them. They should be taught the modified cursive form, known as the DeNealian alphabet, which is a cross between script and print.

Left-handed children should be encouraged to hold their pencils at least 2 centimeters or more (a little less than an inch) away from the tip so that they can more easily see what they are writing. Use pencil grips that are molded to fit the shape of the thumb and the finger. These grips fit over all pens and can help children to develop the proper grip. Encourage the children to write lightly and avoid too tight a grip.

Because left-handers have to push rather than pull a pen or pencil across the page, softer pencils can be helpful. It is also a good idea to experiment with different types of pens until you find one that rolls smoothly. Left-handed fountain pens are now available with angled nibs that are less likely to catch on the paper.

Paper should always be placed to the left of the body's center and may be tilted clockwise at an angle of 20 to 30 degrees. This should help to bring the hand into the correct writing position underneath the writing line.

> Get your child pencil grips, which are molded to fit the shape of the thumb and finger and help children to develop the proper writing grip.

However, I know many lefties who prefer not to tilt the paper this way. As long as your lefty can see what they're writing, this approach is fine. Paper should be supported by the right hand, which should be placed in the middle or toward the right-hand edge of the paper, rather than directly below the writing line.

Lefties should always be seated on the left side of double desks or next to another left-hander to prevent them from bumping elbows with right-handers. Once a lefty is positioned properly, make certain he or she can see the blackboard without having to twist around.

Desks or tables that are too low can encourage raised shoulders, which might promote a more hooked hand position.

Additionally, some of your child's right-handed classmates may never have seen or noticed a left-hander before. Until they see another child writing differently or holding a baseball bat with his or her left hand, most children don't think about the issue of handedness at all. And because children can be extremely blunt, they don't always respond to differences the way we might want them to. Of course, you can't follow your child around to make certain his or her lateral preferences are respected and accommodated all the time, but you can prepare him or her for some of the responses left-handedness might elicit from educators and classmates. All children are teased or misunderstood at one time or another; if dealt with gently and intelligently, this teasing or criticism need not leave emotional scars.

## Talking with Your Child's Teachers

For far too long, many educators were unaware of the problems and concerns left-handed children sometimes face, but in the past 10 or 15 years there has been a steadily growing awareness; consequently, the situation has dramatically improved. Nevertheless, it's always a good idea to go to your child's school in the beginning of the school year and get acquainted with the teachers and administrators. Don't interrogate them or treat your first meeting like an interview. Have a dialogue with them about the school, the administrators, and the other children. Ask about their training and experience and try to develop a cordial relationship. If you feel comfortable, talk a little bit about your own life, your work, and family. Let them know that your child is left-handed and ask them questions to determine if they have the necessary left-handed equipment and supplies. After you've

> Get to know your child's teachers so that you have a good rapport with them. This will help when you need to discuss school or learning-related issues specific to your lefty.

developed a positive relationship with your child's teachers, don't be shy about offering suggestions. And keep the relationship alive by visiting the school and calling when you have any questions. Joining the PTA might also prove helpful.

The same advice applies when sending your child to camp. Make sure the counselors and supervisors know your child is a lefty, but don't make a big deal of it. There will surely be other lefties at camp—and I'll lay odds that some of the counselors will be left-handed too. The point is for your child to enjoy him- or herself, not to feel singled out because of one attribute they have.

## More About Handwriting

Although we no longer see teachers in this country trying to force left-handers to write with their right hands, there has recently been a tendency for some teachers to be a bit lax regarding the quality of children's handwriting. This may be the result of a new teaching philosophy that promotes methods and curricula that de-emphasize rote learning of certain skills, such as handwriting and phonics, in favor of activities that are considered more stimulating or more creative. Because of this, many children are not given serious training in proper handwriting skills, and not enough attention is paid to legibility. Some teachers now place more emphasis on self-expression than on how the letters look. In some ways, this trend can work well for lefties, who, at least initially, may not form their letters perfectly. However, in the long run, this is not helpful to most children because they ultimately adopt poor writing habits, which are very difficult to break. Although it may be politically correct for educators to allow children to write illegibly, it can create serious problems for them in the future.

This can be a very thorny issue. I work with a lot of children with dysgraphia (inability or difficulty with writing properly due to a neurodevelopmental problem). In many cases these problems involve only letters and numbers, but some children also have difficulty with shapes. These children, the majority of whom are boys (because boys develop their fine motor skills later than girls do), are literally unable to form written symbols. They can recognize and understand symbols very well; they just can't reproduce them, and their efforts, which can be physically painful, are generally sloppy and illegible. Some of them, though not all, have other problems, such as difficulty with other fine motor skills or spatial problems. They can also be disorganized. Understandably, these children's parents want the teachers to be more liberal with handwriting—they don't want their children penalized on tests or homework because of poor penmanship. But I also work with parents who want the schools to teach their children how to write properly and to reinforce good handwriting habits. So I'm between a rock and a hard place when it comes to this issue.

My own opinion is that, starting in prekindergarten and kindergarten, children should be taught to write correctly and be given the proper training and tools with which to do this. When a child develops good writing habits early, it's win–win for everyone.

Occasionally, a child will be unable to learn to form letters properly because of a neurodevelopmental lag—in other words; the child is truly dysgraphic. In these cases, the child should be assessed by an occupational therapist in kindergarten and given occupational therapy to address the problem. Schools tend not to want to do this because it's costly, but the children are the ones who suffer if these issues aren't addressed.

Teachers and parents need to assess a child's handwriting so that they can address these problems early. The best time to intervene is when a child is between the ages of 5 and 8 years. Once specific motor skills such as writing are ingrained in a child's brain, they are extremely difficult or impossible to change. Of course you should attempt to work with a child who's having difficulty to improve his or her skills, though I would avoid the techniques that require relentless repetition. The idea is not to win penmanship awards; it is to enable the child to develop the basic skills necessary to write legibly. Unfortunately, these efforts aren't always successful. If you recognize or suspect that a child is dysgraphic, you should have him or her evaluated by an occupational therapist or neuropsychologist.

When a child is truly dysgraphic and has difficulty writing legibly, he or she should be given every possible accommodation, including having the teacher accept less than legible handwriting. In cases in which a child seems unable to conquer the problem, you should consider using assistive technologies. If the child requires a computer to do schoolwork, one should be made available. If a child needs to express his or her thoughts verbally, this should also be an option. Children need to be able to express themselves, and every child should be given the opportunity to progress.

Nevertheless, I think that some teachers, in an effort to accommodate those children who might be having trouble, have allowed their standards to slide too far and that many children are not being taught to write properly in the first place. This can make it even more difficult to determine who is really having a problem and who is not. And again, once a child begins to develop a motor memory for these fine skills, it becomes difficult for him or her to make corrections. Writing is a crucial form of communication, and children who write poorly are often embarrassed by it. It's true that learning to write properly may be more difficult for some left-handed children than for some right-handers, but if teachers don't keep the standard consistently high, it is the children who will eventually pay the price.

## Other Potential Problems

What some teachers often do not take into account are the issues of placement of materials and the child's position at his or her desk and in the classroom. There can also be serious problems with certain "bubble format" tests—those tests where the child fills in one of a series of circles. Too often, these tests are set up for right-handed children, and in the cases where a single sheet of paper includes both the questions and answers, there is no simple solution. Parents of both right-handed and left-handed children are constantly complaining about the bubble sheets, but so far the standardized testing companies have not responded at all, and the schools are loath to make accommodations unless they are forced to do so.

Over the years, I have written many letters to teachers requesting that they allow left-handed children with motor problems to write their answers on the same paper where the questions are printed. This is additional work for already overworked teachers, who then have to transfer the answers and fill in the corresponding bubbles, but for the children involved it could mean the difference between a passing grade and a failing one. Although a teacher might not be quite as eager to respond to such a request directly from a parent, your odds of receiving a positive response will undoubtedly improve if you've taken the time to forge a constructive relationship with the teacher from the beginning.

But let me be clear about this: No accommodations are formally made for children regarding standardized testing procedures unless they are proved to have a handicapping condition. Most schools will not make special accommodations without an assessment and a letter from a qualified doctor stating that the child has a disability that entitles him or her to such accommodations. This is unfortunate, but it is how the system presently works. I must prove that my client has some disability, however minor, that makes the taking of standardized tests problematic for him or her. I could say that the child is dysgraphic and can't fill in the bubbles correctly or that the child has a learning disability and needs help taking the exam. Or I could say that the child has a weakness on one side of the body that makes it difficult for him or her to hold the paper with one hand while filling in the bubbles with the other. What all this means is that the child must be evaluated first and shown to have a disability.

The problem is that some of the children who are struggling with these tests do not have actual disabilities (as far as I'm aware, left-handedness is not considered a disability, nor would I ever want it to be so considered), so it's difficult to prove the need for this accommodation. However, sometimes I can get around all this by talking to the teacher or counselors involved at the school.

This is easier to do at private schools than in public schools, but in either case I will try to get someone to assist children who need it when taking standardized tests. Often, younger children will already be getting this assistance from their teachers, who are in the room with them when they take these tests. Older children, however, may be thrown into a large room, and their regular teachers may or may not be present. A nice letter and a phone call from me, or from another psychologist or child education specialist, will sometimes do the trick in getting some assistance.

Of course, this is usually less of a problem when the child is taking non-standardized tests (midterms, finals, etc.). In these cases, the teacher is usually in the room with the children, and I can usually get the teacher to help the child with the various test formats. But again, I am technically required to write a letter stating why the child needs this assistance.

My experience has been that most teachers do try their best to make accommodations for their students. And in spite of the technical requirements, parents have every right to ask their children's teachers to allow their left-handed children to place their tests and bubble sheets in whatever configuration is comfortable for them and to see to it that they have normal desks on which to work on these forms.

Modular desks also pose a problem. Except in those cases in which a neutral style of desk is used, at least 10 percent of the desks in each classroom should be left-handed desks—desks that enable left-handers to lean on their left arms when they write. Schools should also make pens and pencils with left-handed grips and left-handed rulers available to those children who require them. If your child's teacher is unable to see to it that these items are made available, you may need to go directly to the principal to ask for help.

Another problem most left-handers are forced to contend with in school is spiral binders. A left-handed child who has to use a standard binder is likely to find it difficult and terribly uncomfortable. The metal spring that

---

If double desks are used in your child's classroom, he or she should be seated next to another lefty to avoid elbow bumping.

---

holds the binder together is positioned so that he or she cannot help but struggle with it when trying to write on the proper side of the paper. Parents are generally expected to purchase their children's binders, and though it may require a little more time and energy for the parents of a left-handed child to obtain the proper tools, doing so is well worth the additional effort. Of course, you can take an ordinary binder and write on the opposite side of the paper so that the spring is out of the child's way, but this will mean that when the work is placed in a notebook, it will be displayed on the left side of the rings. Some teachers might penalize a child for handing in work this way. Whatever approach you choose, by addressing these issues you will most likely be increasing your child's speed and efficiency and helping to reduce his or her potential frustration.

Sports and music are two more areas where both the equipment and the training are critical to a child's success. Unfortunately, many well-meaning and intelligent music instructors and gym teachers are still unaware of the issues related to left-handedness. But caring, competent teachers will be eager to learn ways in which they can foster the development of all their students. By passing on the knowledge you've gained and the strategies and techniques you've developed for teaching your lefty, you will be helping your own child as well as those who

Lefties have a hard time using binders; they should use regular notebooks, folders, and pads instead.

share his or her lateral preferences. You will find more detailed information about Sports and Music below and in Chapter Eight.

## Choosing / Finding Appropriate Supplies

### School

There was a time, not that long ago, when, depending on where you lived and what your economic circumstances were, you might have had no choice but to accept the right-handed supplies and equipment your local school had to offer. Now, thanks to a growing awareness of the issue of laterality and the increasing availability of left-handed supplies, this situation is beginning to improve. If your school does not yet stock these items and you are unable to convince school officials to do so, you can purchase them in school supply stores, through catalogs, or online.

You can purchase special pencil grips for left-handers and right-handers from a variety of sources. By affixing these rubber grips to standard pens or pencils, you can increase your child's comfort and efficiency. Another option is to purchase left-handed pens and pencils that are designed to accommodate the left-handed writing positions without the use of separate grips. Many of these left-handed pens also use ink that dries quickly so that it will be less likely to smear and smudge as your child's hand follows his or her script across the page. Some of the pencils use a special smudge-resistant lead. There are also rulers that read from right to left, enabling left-handers to read the numbers while they work without having to cross their hands.

Left-handed pencil sharpeners and scissors are relatively inexpensive and can help to reduce frustration and the sense of awkwardness that might otherwise develop. To eliminate the difficulties and discomforts I outlined in the section above, you can now purchase left-handed spiral notebooks, with the wire spiral on the right, where it won't get in the way of the writer's wrist, and the holes for placement in a standard three-ring notebook on the left. With these binders your left-handed child can write in comfort and then transfer his or her finished work to a traditional three-hole notebook.

More and more schools are using computers to prepare children to compete in an increasingly high-tech society. This can actually be an aid to those left-handers who can't seem to fully conquer their difficulties with handwriting. In the same way that you would arrange a common workstation in your home, you should make certain the computers in your child's school are lefty friendly. Left-handed keyboards, with the numeric and arrow keypads on the left, are now available, and there is a growing selection of left-handed mice and joysticks from which to choose.

I have found most of the supplies I've needed at the local teachers' supply stores, but there are other options if you can't find what you want locally. There are a number of companies who sell left-handed school supplies through mail order and on the Internet. You will find a listing in the Resources section of this book.

## Sports

Whether it's in the classroom, on the school playground, or in the gym, your child will be expected to play and compete with his or her right-handed classmates. If your school doesn't provide them and you are unable to persuade teachers and administrators that it's in their best interests to obtain them, you can purchase left-handed sports equipment, such as catcher's mitts and fielder's gloves, from a variety of sources. Thanks to the incredible successes of athletes such as Sandy Koufax, Monica Seles, Jimmy Connors, Dorothy Hamill, Babe Ruth, Martina Navratilova, and Larry Bird, we know that left-handedness should never be viewed as a handicap in sports.

## Music

If your child expresses an interest in music, you will want to see to it that he or she has access to instruments and training that won't cause additional difficulty. Most guitars and bass guitars are right-handed instruments, but there are dozens of manufacturers who now produce left-handed versions of those same instruments. It used to be that these left-handed instruments were considerably more expensive than the right-handed versions, but that's not the case any longer. Of course with certain instruments, such as woodwinds and some brass, the solution may not be so simple as finding a left-handed instrument—they simply don't exist. And there is no such thing as a left-handed piano.

Although it might seem simpler in some cases to steer your left-handed child toward a musical instrument that isn't going to fight against him or her, you may not be able to deter an enthusiastic child, and you may not want to. With interest, and a little natural ability, there is a very good chance that your child will find his or her way. Remember that some of the most talented and successful musicians have found their genius in the struggle with adversity. Jimi Hendrix didn't have the luxury of a left-handed instrument. In fact, there are those who feel this challenge may have played an important part in the unique style he developed. And, in spite of his left-handedness, and the total hearing loss he experienced later in life, Beethoven's incomparable genius continues to inspire music lovers the world over.

In addition to the question of musical equipment, there is the sticky issue of training. With string instruments, such as the electric bass and the guitar, the ideal solution might be something as simple as having the teacher sit across from the student to create a mirror image. Of course it would be great if you were able to find a left-handed instructor for your left-handed child, but unfortunately, that's not very likely. As long as your child and his or her teachers understand the potential impediments, they should be able to find ways to work around them. Paul McCartney, Natalie Cole, and Wynton Marsalis are just a few more of the many left-handed musicians who have done quite well for themselves in a predominantly right-handed world.

The evidence is convincing and the news is quite good. Given a chance and a level playing field, your left-hander will likely flourish and excel intellectually, athletically, and emotionally.

## Famous Lefty U.S. Politicos

- Bill Bradley, senator, Rhodes scholar, basketball star
- McGeorge Bundy, presidential advisor
- Steve Forbes, businessman, publisher, former presidential hopeful
- Benjamin Franklin, statesman, author, scientist
- Ruth Bader Ginsberg, Supreme Court Justice
- Daniel Inouye, senator
- Anthony Kennedy, Supreme Court Justice
- Robert S. McNamara, Secretary of Defense
- Oliver North, marine colonel and White House aide
- H. Ross Perot, businessman, founder of the Reform Party
- William Perry, Secretary of Defense
- Nelson Rockefeller, former vice president
- Hugh Scott, senator
- Robert Wagner, former New York City mayor
- Henry Wallace, former vice president

# Chapter Eight

# Recreation and Your Lefty

Whether your left-handed child dreams of being an athlete, a musician, a chef, or a carpenter, he or she may be faced with regulations and equipment that were fashioned with someone else in mind. Even the settings for some recreational activities are designed with the assumption that those using them will be right-handed. And then there is the issue of instruction. In spite of all of this, I would enthusiastically encourage all left-handed children, and adults for that matter, to pursue their dreams with hope and confidence. If a child's talents and interests are nurtured at an early age, it will be much easier for him or her to tackle any obstacles that might arise.

# The Left-Handed Athlete

For years there was simply no such thing as a left-handed golf club. You will seldom if ever see a left-handed second base player, third base player, or shortstop. And although there are still regulations banning left-handers from playing polo, the situation for left-handed athletes has improved dramatically. Indeed, it seems that when offered proper training and the opportunity to play, lefties often excel at sports. Baseball is probably the first sport most people think of when the subject of left-handed athletes is raised, but even in sports such as bowling and billiards, where handedness would appear to be irrelevant, lefties are often overrepresented.

## Differences Between Right- and Left-Handed Equipment

Some of the differences between right- and left-handed equipment are obvious. Left-handed catcher's mitts go on the right hand. (You may have to forget about hand-me-downs.) Left-handed golf clubs are basically the mirror image of right-handed clubs. The finger holes in left-handed bowling balls are arranged to accommodate the fingers of the left hand rather than the right.

But in some sports, such as bicycling, the differences aren't quite so apparent. It may not be possible to change the position of the shifters on most modern bikes, but you can easily reverse the brake cables so that the left hand, generally the stronger hand in a left-handed person, activates the rear brake and the weaker right hand activates the front. In many sports, such as basketball, football, and tennis, the equipment will be nondiscriminatory. In those sports that require it, left-handed equipment is increasingly accessible. There was a time, not so long ago, when lefties were forced to pay a lot more for their equipment than righties paid for theirs. These days most left-handed equipment is comparably priced to or just slightly more expensive than right-handed equipment.

## How to Instruct

It would probably be ideal if all left-handed youngsters had the luxury of talented left-handed instructors and coaches, but it isn't a very likely scenario. Fortunately, there are alternatives for children who aren't that lucky. If you're right-handed and you want to coach your lefty you may find that you have to take some extra time, but what better way is there to spend time with your child? And you may get a workout in the bargain!

One technique you might try when teaching your left-handed child how to hold a baseball bat or to throw a ball is to stand facing him or her to create a mirror image as a visual guide. Obviously you will want to keep enough distance between you and your child so that no one is injured. Or you might try to learn how to perform with your left hand the tasks you want to teach your left-handed child. Certainly if your right hand were

Almost every sport is open to lefties these days. There's no need to discourage your child from playing or becoming involved in any athletic activity. Plus, being a member of a team is great preparation for life!

injured you would find some way to do whatever you had to do. The fact is, you might find it an interesting and educational, if somewhat frustrating, exercise.

However you choose to proceed in training your left-handed child, remember how important it is to be observant, to be aware of his or her distinctive differences, and to do your best to accommodate them. Still, as is the case with many of the other issues I've addressed, it is equally important not to think of left-handedness as a handicap or to assume that it will necessarily present problems. To be hypervigilant or overbearing can sometimes be as counterproductive as being inattentive.

And it's crucial to remember that your left-handed son or daughter may play one sport left-handed and another right-handed. This tendency in left-handed individuals is still a mystery but should certainly not be discouraged.

## Left-Handedness as a Competitive Strategy

There is really no question that left-handedness can be an advantage in certain sports, particularly in sports such as tennis, where one player competes directly with another, or baseball, where players spend years developing and honing strategies and techniques intended for use against right-handed opponents. In fact, many older baseball stadiums, such as Yankee Stadium in New York, are more conducive to left-handed hitters because the right-field fence is shorter than the left-field fence, giving lefties an advantage when batting toward right field. But though left-handed pitchers and batters are sought after for their edge over their right-handed opponents, there are almost undoubtedly other less obvious advantages to being a left-handed athlete.

For instance, it may be that some lefties have the benefit of superior spatial abilities. Briefly, there are two major types of spatial abilities—intrapersonal and extrapersonal. Intrapersonal spatial abilities develop early in life and are responsible for the understanding of where your body ends and another one begins, where your limbs are in space, judging distances between you and your environment, knowing left from right, and so forth. An advantage in these areas could certainly have a positive impact in sports in which positioning is important or where there is a target of some kind.

Understanding extrapersonal space is a more complex, more abstract cognitive ability. Extrapersonal spatial abilities enable you to understand how other objects are related to each other in space, how pieces make up a whole, and what will happen if you rearrange those pieces. Someone with superior extrapersonal spatial skills might be able to visualize what an object will look like just by seeing the different pieces or might be able to translate a two-dimensional form into a three-dimensional replica of that form. Although the highest form of spatial ability is used in such areas as mathematics and architecture, these skills can also be a great advantage in other areas, such as landscaping, and probably in such games as billiards, in which a grasp of geometry can play a significant role.

It may also be that because their right and left brains often communicate particularly well, some left-handers possess a sort of corporeal unity—their motor skills, spatial skills, and strategic thought processes are able to combine forces in an almost seamless cooperative effort. Whether it's through a conscious effort to take advantage of the distinctive nature of left-handedness or because of the subtle differences in the way lefties' brains are wired, it seems clear that left-handedness can be at least one element in an athlete's success.

## Baseball

Left-handed hitters and switch-hitters are highly prized. The former have a clear advantage because the majority of pitchers are right-handed, and a left-handed batter can more easily spot a breaking ball. Switch-hitters have the ability to hit right-handed or left-handed, depending on the pitcher they are facing. Of course, your lefty may be more comfortable batting right-handed. In fact, close to 40 percent of lefties throw and bat right-handed. It may be that left-handed children and children with left-handed parents are better able to learn to switch-hit than most righties. I don't think anyone has ever done a study on this, but being left-handed or having parents who are left-handed does raise the possibility that the right-handed gene is absent. This means that hand dominance can develop either way in these children. By all means, if it looks as though your child is leaning in this direction, encourage left-handed or switch-hitting.

The fact is that some of the greatest hitters in baseball history have hit left-handed: Babe Ruth, Lou Gehrig, Ted Williams, Stan Musial, Yogi Berra, Mickey Mantle, Reggie Jackson, Willie McCovey, Willie Stargell, George Brett, Rod Carew, and Pete Rose, to name a few. There have also been some rare successful switch-hitters. Mickey Mantle may be the most well known example, but Pete Rose was also a talented switch-hitter, and Bernie Williams and Roberto Alomar are two current examples of players who have honed this rare skill.

Approximately 30 percent of major-league pitchers are left-handed. Sandy Koufax, a famous lefty, was perhaps the greatest pitcher in the history of the sport. Between 1961 and 1967, during which time he was given the Cy Young Award three times, he pitched four no-hitters, a statistic unparalleled to this day. He was

---

In baseball, left-handed pitchers are highly prized because they have an edge over their right-handed opponents. If your child shows skill or an interest in this aspect of the game, encourage him or her to develop his or her talent. Mastering a skill will enhance your child's self-esteem.

also something of a mystery to the public, always very uncomfortable about talking about himself and shunning the limelight throughout his life. Other left-handed pitchers of note are Whitey Ford (the best pitcher ever for the New York Yankees) and Steve Carlton.

If your child shows interest and skill in baseball, be encouraging and see to it that he or she practices a lot. One of my teenage clients, Joanna, is the star pitcher on her baseball team. Of course she is left-handed. When she told me how well she was doing, I thought it was the coolest thing a girl could do. I was even a little envious because I was never coordinated enough to even throw a ball correctly.

Surprisingly (because the odds are against it), there have been many families where both father and son have played major league baseball. Sandy Alomar, who hit left-handed but threw right-handed, played second base during the late 1960s and early 1970s. Currently, Sandy Alomar Jr., who throws and bats right-handed, plays for the Chicago White Sox, and his brother, Roberto Alomar, a right-handed switch-hitter, plays for the Cleveland Indians. Sandy Sr. was considered an average player, but Roberto in particular is recognized as one of the best players in baseball.

Ken Griffey Jr., who bats and throws left-handed and is expected to break the all-time home run record set by Hank Aaron, is currently regarded the best player in baseball. His father, Ken Griffey, Sr., also batted and threw left but was considered to be a good player. Barry Bonds, who bats and throws left-handed, is nearly on the same level as Griffey, Jr. Barry's father, Bobby, who batted and threw right-handed, was considered among the game's better players, though certainly not as good as his left-handed son.

Interestingly enough, Mickey Mantle had a son who attempted to make it as a major-league ball player but who never made it to the major leagues. Also, Yogi Berra had a right-handed son who was in the major leagues briefly but who was just an average player. Like his famous father, he was a catcher.

The majority of left-handed hitters have been out-fielders. My husband tells me that in 30 years of watching baseball he can't recall ever seeing a catcher, third-base player, shortstop, or second-base player who threw left. I think a major part of this is that they are probably encouraged to be outfielders or first-base players early on in their training.

In fact, left-handed children are often forced to spend much of their time in the outfield because the sense is that they will be at a disadvantage in other positions. The only infield positions often covered by left-handed players are first base or pitcher. From second base, third base, or shortstop, they have to turn in order to throw toward first. Still, I feel that all children should be given every opportunity to play different positions, though this is not likely to happen unless you have a very open-minded coach. However, don't be discouraged as a parent if the coach refuses to allow your child to play another infield position such as shortstop or catcher, because, as a lefty, your child still has a major advantage as a hitter or pitcher. Because of their unique ability to face right-handed opponents, left-handed baseball players tend to have a better chance to excel.

## Basketball

Because the court is symmetrical and players are able to move around and use both hands during play, instruction is the major issue left-handers are confronted with in the sport of basketball. Spatial skills will certainly come in handy on the basketball court, and there may be a slight additional advantage in terms of the other players' conditioning after years of facing other right-handed opponents. Otherwise, lefties should be on an even keel with their right-handed counterparts.

## Billiards

Cue sticks are neither right- nor left-handed and pool tables are symmetrical. Outside of the issue of training, lefties should have no more trouble learning to play pool than righties.

## Bowling

This is a sport in which equipment is critical. Left-handed bowling balls are available for purchase, but your local bowling alley may not offer them for use by the public. If this is the case, and the management can't be convinced to make them available, you, as a parent, may be forced to buy a left-handed bowling ball. Also, your lefty may want to start off on his or her left foot. If you or your child's instructor is aware of these issues, they shouldn't present serious problems for your young bowler.

## Football

Left-handed-throwing professional quarterbacks are very rare, but then there are only about thirty teams, and the skill level required to be a starting pro quarterback is quite high. Steve Young, who played on the San Francisco 49ers, is probably the best example. In fact, he was widely considered to be one of the most accurate quarterbacks in history. Ken Stabler, who played for the Oakland Raiders, was also an incredibly talented player. Currently, Michael Vick, who was selected out of college by the Atlanta Falcons, is recognized as having a very strong arm as well as perhaps having the greatest running skills of any quarterback in the history of the game. The good news is that handedness appears to be virtually irrelevant in the other positions in this sport. I haven't found any statistics regarding left-handed football players, but with the exception of the position of quarterback, lefties are probably as common and as successful as in any other sport.

## Golf

For a number of years, left-handed golf clubs were simply not available. Bob Charles, author of *The Bob Charles Left-Hander's Golf Book*, was the first left-handed golfer ever to win a PGA tournament event. That was in 1964. It was 10 years later that Sam Adams became the second. Ernie Gonzales, Russ Cochran, and Phil Mickelson are the only other golfers I know of who have successfully played left-handed golf. Today there is an organization known as the National Association of Left-Handed Golfers, and left-handed golf clubs are available to anyone who wants to purchase them. In golf, as in so many sports, there is no reason a left-handed player can't excel with the proper equipment and training.

## Tennis

Because tennis is played on a symmetrical court and the equipment is not designed for a particular hand, left-handers are not forced to start out at a disadvantage. Additionally, tennis involves a lot of movement and coordination, so lefties may in fact have some intrinsic advantage over righties. Add to that the fact that right-handers have to alter their competitive strategies dramatically when facing left-handed opponents and you might begin to understand the successes of so many left-handed tennis players. Of course I'm not suggesting that John McEnroe, Jimmy Connors, and Monica Seles aren't all highly skilled, well-disciplined players. I'm simply saying that it might not be unreasonable to attribute some small part of their success to their handedness and all that comes with it. With capable instruction and some natural talent, your left-handed child could prove to be a skilled tennis player.

## Wrestling

In the sport of wrestling, as in so many of the other sports I've mentioned, left-handed players, by virtue of their relative scarcity, can be a source of confusion and frustration for their right-handed opponents. Where lefties may be at a disadvantage in certain holds or positions, the great majority of their opponents will be right-handed. Lefties will almost undoubtedly have the advantage when it comes to hours of experience competing against an opponent with dissimilar lateral preferences.

# Music

There is no such thing as a left-handed grand piano. With all that goes into constructing a piano, there may never be. Consequently, there have not been many left-handed pianists, though there have been some wonderful ones. Although several of his portraits show him holding a pen in his right hand, classical pianist and composer Ludwig van Beethoven is widely believed to have been left-handed. Jazz pianist and composer Erroll Garner was also a lefty, as was Carl Philipp Emanuel Bach, the third son of Johann Sebastian Bach and an influential harpsichordist and composer in his own right. The late Glenn Gould, an enormously skilled, world-renowned classical pianist, was left-handed.

This is all the more impressive because in most piano music, whether classical, jazz, or rock, the great majority of the intricate passages are played by the right hand while the left hand lays a foundation, playing chords, bass lines, or a simpler counterpoint to the flashy work the right hand is doing. Consequently, the right hand generally has to be more nimble, faster, and stronger than the left. But what the above list of left-handed pianists clearly demonstrates is that talent, passion, desire, and commitment can overcome even the most potentially stifling obstacles.

Like keyboards, many woodwind, brass, and string instruments can present problems to lefties, though possibly to a somewhat lesser degree. To the best of my knowledge, there are no left-handed vibraphones, and although you can order a custom-made left-handed violin, that would be an enormous expense to incur, particularly when you have no idea how long a young child's interest is going to last. This doesn't mean that a lefty can't become a skilled violinist or vibraphonist. It simply means that lefties might have to contend with some additional obstacles in learning to play these instruments.

For example, a violinist fingers with the left hand, but the right hand does the "work," which is with the bow. In fact, the act of moving the bow across the instrument requires more strength than fingering. It's also somewhat awkward for lefties to play the sax, clarinet, and flute, but it's by no means impossible. In terms of a sax and clarinet, both hands are used. The left hand is usually on the top of the instrument and the right hand is on the bottom. There are also side valves to work. A lefty wouldn't necessarily have to cross hands to play these instruments—just practice a little harder than a right-handed

Most major music stores now stock or are able to order left-handed instruments. Learning to play an instrument is a wonderful hobby too. Making music promotes creativity, coordination, fine motor skills, and teamwork.

person who didn't feel as awkward holding the instrument. A flute presents a similar set of challenges, but again, if a child is really drawn to an instrument and to making music, especially at a young age, nothing can stop him or her from playing and learning.

Fortunately, not all musical instruments have these potential built-in limitations. Most major guitar manufacturers now produce a variety of left-handed instruments, the majority of which are priced the same as or just slightly higher than the comparable right-handed instruments. The trombone can be played left-handed without any difficulty, whereas with drums, the necessary adjustments are merely a matter of positioning. It takes no more than a couple minutes to switch a drum set from a right-handed configuration to a left-handed one. Remember, Wynton Marsalis learned to play on a standard right-handed instrument. His incredible facility and success with the trumpet would suggest that left-handedness has not deterred him a bit, or if it has indeed been an obstacle, he certainly has made the most of it. In fact, it's not all that difficult to play trumpet left-handed. There are a few things about a trumpet's design that may make playing left-handed awkward. For example, the pinky ring that a player uses to support the trumpet while playing is placed on the instrument's right hand side. The tubing is also narrower on the right side of the trumpet, so if you are playing it lefty, you have to reach a little further around the wider tubing on the left side to reach the valves.

## Where to Get Left-Handed Instruments and Equipment

Although it wasn't true before the early 1990s, most major music stores now stock or are able to quickly special-order left-handed instruments. This may be due, in part, to the many well-known left-handed musicians I've mentioned. There are also a number of online music stores that keep a variety of left-handed instruments in stock, such as www.musiciansfriend.com.

## How to Instruct

If a child seems to have a real interest and a hint of natural ability, he or she is likely to find a way to conquer virtually any obstacle that appears. Still, as a parent, it is natural for you to want to keep these obstacles to a minimum, to give your child every opportunity to succeed. If you're fortunate enough to find a left-handed instructor, your child may indeed find it easier to learn, but a simple awareness of a student's lateral preferences, and the issues that might arise, should go a long way toward making the learning experience a productive and positive one.

## Cooking

The great majority of modern kitchen utensils are designed for use with either hand. Many ladles and frying pans now have pour spouts on both sides, and most of the newer mixing cups have measuring lines and information on either side. Some knives have serrated edges on both sides, and most modern peelers can be used with either hand.

As discussed earlier, as soon as a child is old enough, regardless of his or her lateral preferences, you should train him or her in the proper use of knives and other potentially dangerous kitchen implements to avoid accidents. You will probably find some basic instruction in the use of kitchen knives and utensils in any good comprehensive cookbook. Assume the instructions are intended for right-handed users (unless the book indicates otherwise), use the appropriate utensils for your lefty, and simply substitute the motions of the left hand for those of the right and vice versa.

### *Where to Get Equipment*

Because of increasing consumer demand, many of the modern utensils you can find in your local stores are designed for use with either hand. If you have trouble locating an ambidextrous or left-handed model of a particular utensil, try talking with the store manager. He or she may be familiar with this issue and therefore eager to respond to your requests. But if you can't find what you're looking for and you don't get a helpful response from store managers, there are options. There are numerous left-handed retail shops scattered throughout the United States and abroad. Most of these businesses offer mail-order purchase of everything from school supplies to sports equipment to kitchen utensils. See the Resources section of this book for a comprehensive list of these shops.

## Instruction

An individual's lateral preferences have little bearing on most of the skills required by performers of the culinary arts. Equipment and kitchen layout are issues that may have to be addressed, but beyond that, instruction is the only real concern. This is another area where as long as the instructor is aware of the potential obstacles of equipment and placement, there should be no problem. It may be that most diagrams and instructions in cookbooks are laid out for right-handed readers, but by simply reversing the right hand for the left when necessary, that issue can be easily resolved. Chances are that most of the necessary adjustments will come naturally.

# Art

In general, the visual arts offer little in the way of obstacles to lefties. In fact, judging by the high percentage of left-handers in our art schools, it would seem that they have an inherent interest and faculty in art. I knew a student in Boston whose left-handed mother was a well-known artist. She painted left-handed but sculpted with her right hand. I never understood this. It just goes to show that the brain is very mysterious.

Whether there is a genetic link between handedness and artistic ability or this interest is a consequence of the creative force needed to survive in a left-handed world, any creative interest should be encouraged in children, regardless of their lateral preferences. By honing manual dexterity, and hand–eye coordination, activities such as painting, drawing, and sculpting can help children with many other skills. Additionally, these disciplines can encourage creativity and self-expression. The question of whether left-handed children are in fact more creative than righties will probably be debated for years to come, but there is no question that nurturing a child's creative impulses and interests can be a positive and rewarding endeavor for everyone involved.

The left-handed artist's workspace might require minor alterations, but the majority of the tools and equipment he or she will utilize will not have a right-handed bias. Training is by far the most potentially troublesome issue your lefty is likely to face when attempting disciplines such as drawing, painting, and sculpting. In those cases in which an instructor might normally place his or her right hand over a student's right hand, adjustments might be necessary. When possible, the right-handed instructor should attempt to use his or her left hand to guide the left-handed child. In some cases, it may be a good idea for the instructor to stand across from the student and have him or her mirror the different grips and motions. Again, a simple awareness of the issues involved can make the difference between a smooth road and a rough one.

The same is true in terms of most crafts. Because most people are right-handed, crafts are generally taught by right-handed instructors. Additionally, most instructions are designed for the right-handed majority. In some cases left-handers may need to reverse the instructions for a particular project, using the left hand when the instructions say right and vice versa. Equipment, on the other hand, doesn't present any serious problems in these areas. Left-handed or ambidextrous scissors are now easy to find, and most of the other tools involved in sewing, crocheting, needlepoint, and knitting aren't designed for a particular hand.

## Sewing

Instead of scissors, many people now use rotary cutters, cutting tools that don't have an inherent handedness bias—they are like small pizza wheels but with very sharp interchangeable blades for straight cutting, pinking, and so on. Most sewing machines are configured for right-handed users, but because you can generally sit on either side of the table to use them and you can place the presser foot on either side, there should be no real problem.

## Pottery

Many modern pottery wheels have an option for a reversing switch (a switch that can reverse the direction of the wheel's spin). But the fact is that whether you are right- or left-handed doesn't usually affect whether you throw clay clockwise or counterclockwise. It depends more on the country in which you learned. Some countries, such as Japan, have a history of throwing counterclockwise. For those who have learned to throw counterclockwise or those who like to trim in the opposite direction from the one in which they throw, a reversing switch can be useful. These are two Web sites where you can purchase pottery wheels with reversing switches: www.bigceramicstore.com/Supplies/wheels/wheels.htm and www.clayartcenter.com/wheel_lock.htm.

## Woodworking

Tools and instruction can both present problems for left-handed woodworkers. Although the situation has been gradually improving, power tools can often be problematic for left-handed users. As I stated in Chapter Six, it is probably wise to treat any tool as though it presents a potential danger. Look at the list in Chapter Six and inspect and evaluate all tools before training your child to use them.

## A Final Thought on Recreation

Some children will excel at one activity, whereas others will have success with another; most of the time this will have very little to do with their lateral preferences. But whether a child has a special talent in one area or another is far less important than that he or she enjoys the process. Of course, children tend to prefer doing things that they're good at to those things that present difficulties. But as long as your child is learning or enjoying an activity, and as long as your child's safety is ensured, his or her interest and involvement should be encouraged and nurtured. It may take some time and a little experimentation, but children tend to find their way.

### *Famous Lefty Athletes*

#### Racing
- Johnny Herbert (Formula One)
- Terry Labonte (NASCAR)
- Valentino Rossi (motorcycle)
- Ayrton Senna (Formula One)
- Karl Wendlinger (Formula One)

#### Baseball
*Pitchers*
- Whitey Ford
- Lefty Grove
- Ron Guidry

- Steve Howe
- Randy Johnson
- Sandy Koufax
- Al Leiter

*Players*
- Harold Baines
- Yogi Berra
- Barry Bonds
- George Brett
- Lou Brock
- Brett Butler
- Will Clark
- Ty Cobb
- Lenny Dykstra
- John Franco
- Ken Griffey Jr.
- Tony Gwynn
- Rickey Henderson
- Reggie Jackson
- "Shoeless" Joe Jackson
- Wally Joyner
- David Justice
- Tommy Lasorda (baseball manager)
- Dave Martinez
- Don Mattingly
- John Olerud
- Paul O'Neil
- Babe Ruth
- Casey Stengel

- Darryl Strawberry
- Fernando Valenzuela
- Lou Whitaker
- Ted Williams

## Football

- Frankie Albert
- Terry Baker
- Mark Brunell (quarterback)
- Bobby Douglass
- Norman "Boomer" Esiason
- Jim Del Gaizon
- David Humm
- Paul McDonald
- Scott Mitchell
- Gayle Sayers
- Allie Sherman (coach)
- Ken Stabler
- Steve Young
- Jim Zorn

## Basketball

- Walter Berry
- Larry Bird
- Dave Cowens
- Adrian Dantley
- Charles "Lefty" Driesell
- Mark Eaton
- Gail Goodrich
- Ron Kellogg

- Toni Kukoc
- Bob Lanier
- Brad Lohaus
- Dick Motta
- Chris Mullen
- Sam Perkins
- Digger Phelps
- Willis Reed
- Guy Rodgers
- Bill Russell
- Wayman Tisdale
- Bill Walton
- Lenny Wilkins
- Manuel Zuleta

## Golf
- Bonny Bryant
- Bob Charles
- Russ Cochran
- Connie Decker

## Billiards
- Steve Mizerak Jr.

## Soccer
- Jans van Breukelen
- Johan Cruyff
- Willem van Hanegem
- Diego Armando Maradona
- Hernan Medford
- Pelé (Edson Arantes do Nascimento)

- Romário
- Hugo Sanchez
- Richard Witschge

## Bowling
- Bill Allen
- Earl Anthony
- Mike Aulby
- Steve Cook
- Patty Costello
- Dave Davis
- Tish Johnson
- Johnny Petraglia
- Andy Varipapa

## Olympic Sports
- Francis X. Gorman (diving)
- Dorothy Hamill (skating)
- Bruce Jenner (decathlon)
- Nikita Kohloff (wrestling)
- Greg Louganis (diving)
- Mark Spitz (swimming)

## Boxing
- Carmen Basilio
- James "Gentleman Jim" Corbett
- Marvin Hagler
- Oscar De La Hoya
- Reggie Johnson
- Rafael "Bazooka" Limon
- Freddie Miller

- Jacker Patterson
- Pernell "Sweet Pea" Whitaker

## Hockey
- Tom Barrasso
- Phil Esposito
- Cam Neely
- Terry Sawchuk
- Roman Turek

## Tennis
- Norman Brookes
- Kenneth Carlsen
- Jimmy Connors
- Courtney De Mone
- Guy Forget
- Andres Gomez (Santos)
- Goran Ivanisevic
- Rod Laver
- Henri Leconte
- John McEnroe
- Thomas Muster
- Martina Navratilova (ambidextrous)
- Manuel Orantes
- Niki Pilic
- Renee Richards
- Marcello Chino Rios
- Monica Seles
- Roscoe Tanner
- Guillermo Vilas
- Mark Woodforde

# Chapter
# Nine

## Possible Problems and How to Overcome Them

The fact is that all children are subject to difficulties of one kind or another. Some children experience difficulties involving motor skills (skills related to the movement of their bodies and limbs); others might have trouble with language skills (speaking, comprehension, reading, writing, etc.). These are critical areas for early learning. Occasional illness is an unfortunate fact of life, and accidents can happen to anyone, young or old. Whether your child is left-handed or right-handed, you will want to do everything in your power to reduce the likelihood of problems and to help him or her if and when they can't be averted. It may be that for one reason or another, left-handers are more prone to certain types of difficulties than are right-handers, or it may be that because of the increased scrutiny to which left-handers are sometimes subjected, their problems are more readily noticed. Most likely it's a combination of the two. Although it is helpful to understand the causes, it is even more critical that we recognize our children's problems early so that we can address them properly and immediately.

## Stammering and Stuttering

Over the years, several studies have suggested a link between left-handedness and stuttering. Though there is still some debate regarding the connection, the most convincing theories are the ones that suggest that these involuntary behaviors are sometimes caused by attempts to force a child to switch handedness. I have seen no evidence whatsoever suggesting that left-handers are inherently more likely to stutter than right-handers. If your child does indeed demonstrate a tendency to stutter at some point in his or her development, try not to react to it too much. This could aggravate the problem. Instead, simply point it out and ask the child to speak more slowly. The fact is that many preschoolers stutter at one time or another; possibly because they have a lot to say and can't get it out or are having difficulty finding the right words to express themselves. If the stuttering persists and begins to affect the child in school, I would advise a consultation with a speech therapist.

The good news is that mild and even moderate stuttering is relatively easy to treat. And though it may cause

> Speech, language, and learning specialists can help make dramatic improvements in a left-handed child's development.

you some concern, you should know that stuttering in preschool is not a predictor of future reading and writing problems.

## Illness

### Differences in Lefties' Susceptibilities

Although all children are susceptible to injuries and illness, some left-handed children face a unique set of potential problems. For instance, left-handers are slightly more prone to allergies and asthma than right-handers are.

Although you can't prevent a child from developing allergies and you can't completely eliminate the risk of an asthma attack, you can look for signs that there is a problem and take steps to lessen your child's potential discomfort. Congestion, sneezing, red eyes, and itchy skin are among the indications that your child may be suffering with an allergy. In many situations, the solution is a fairly simple one. There may be something in your environment to which your child has an increased sensitivity, or the allergy may be seasonal. It could be a detergent or a family pet, or it might be a particular fabric or a food. Consult your pediatrician if your child shows signs of an allergic reaction; he or she can help

Research suggests that left-handers are slightly more prone to allergies and asthma than right-handers are.

determine the cause or causes. If the allergy is to something you can't remove from the environment, there are medications that can help reduce the symptoms and increase your child's comfort.

Asthma is a respiratory disease that is generally characterized by sudden attacks of labored breathing, coughing, wheezing, and chest constriction. Often it can be triggered by allergies, though that isn't always the case. Asthma attacks range from relatively mild (a dry cough) to severe (all of the above symptoms in acute form over an extended period of time). For those asthmas that are triggered by dust or other allergies, preventative measures (removal of the offending substance) can go a long way toward reducing the frequency and severity of the attacks. In other cases, medication may be required. Again, if you see, or believe you see, symptoms of asthma, consult a pediatrician.

## Differences in the Way Lefties Get Sick

As odd as it may sound, recent studies have shown that lefties even get sick differently from righties. Although it seems clear that left-handers tend to be more prone to allergies and asthma than right-handers, there are areas where lefties have a clear advantage. As mentioned earlier, left-handers often recover from stroke more quickly and more fully than right-handers. We know that this is because lefties generally have more adaptable brains than righties. Although no one yet knows why, statistics clearly indicate that left-handed people are less likely to get Alzheimer's disease than are right-handers.

## Accidents

There is really no way around it. All children tend to be clumsy. Sometimes all that's needed is a gentle reminder: "Slow down and think about what you're doing." And there are certainly degrees of clumsiness. Watch your child; compare him or her with other children of a similar age before assuming there is a problem that needs to be addressed. If your child seems to be inherently clumsy and you're convinced it's not just a part of growing up, it may be helpful to have him or her work with an occupational therapist, who can give you exercises and activities to do together at home.

But, as I stated earlier, some of the accidents left-handers have are caused by awkward or untrained use of machinery and equipment designed for right-handers. Awareness, training, and extra caution may be enough to avert any potentially serious accidents. And remember, children are constantly growing and evolving. It takes time to adjust to these changes.

Take extra time when teaching your lefty to use any type of instrument or tool. Before you even introduce an implement to a child, take a careful look at how it is gripped and where the controls are located. Try holding the tool in your left hand and manipulating the controls

> Spend additional time teaching your lefty how to use tools and equipment. Most accidents occur because tools are being used incorrectly or carelessly—not because your child is "naturally clumsy."

to see if the tool can be safely operated by the lefty. Many power tools, such as saws and drills, still have a right-handed bias. Dials and buttons are often positioned for the right-handed majority, and grips are ergonomically designed for the adult male right hand. If you feel a tool cannot be safely held and used in the left hand, don't allow your child to have access to it. And before you allow your child to use any tool, spend whatever time is necessary to be certain he or she is safe, comfortable, and confident with it. I can't emphasize this enough.

## Dyslexia and Lefties

Though there has been some speculation in the scientific community, a direct connection between lateral preferences and dyslexia has never been proven. As with many other questions regarding the workings of the human brain, there is still work to be done. Still, we are learning more every day. For many years, computed tomography (CT) scans were the only tool we had for viewing the living brain. Then, several years ago, we began using magnetic resonance imaging (MRI), which enabled us to get a clearer picture of brain structure. However, this technology still didn't enable us to look at brain activity. The most recent research, which uses a revolutionary technology known as functional MRI, actually allows researchers to observe the human brain in action.

A lot of exciting research is now being conducted to determine the causes of dyslexia and where the problem is located in the brain. What researchers have found is that the brains of those with dyslexia do indeed differ from the brains of the "normal" population, most notably in the language zone in the left side of the brain, known as the planum temporale, which is located in Sylvius' fissure.

This area of the brain is very important to reading because it deals with phonological processing skills—those skills that enable us to hear, discriminate, and manipulate speech sounds. Dyslexia is believed to be related to a weakness in phonological processing skills. In dyslexics, this area is either totally symmetrical on both sides of the brain or slightly larger on the right, whereas in the majority of the normal population this area is predominantly larger on the left side. Lefties also tend to have a more symmetrical planum. Keep in mind, however, that most of this research has been conducted on right-handers. Because scientists believe that the brains of lefties are inherently different from those of right-handers, we don't know if left-handers with a symmetrical planum have an increased tendency toward

---

**A direct connection between left-handedness and dyslexia has never been proven.**

dyslexia. What we do know is that many lefties who have a symmetrical planum can read perfectly well.

## Learning Delays

Because children vary so dramatically, and because they tend to change and grow so quickly, it can sometimes be difficult to determine whether a child is contending with a learning disability or simply doing battle with a transient obstacle. No matter what your child's lateral preferences, there is no reason to assume that he or she will have a problem with learning. In fact, it is far more likely that he or she will be perfectly normal and healthy. Nevertheless, you should keep your eyes and ears open and pay close attention while enjoying your child's growth and development. If you know what to look for, you can begin to address problems before they become more severe.

## When to Seek Professional Help

If your child experiences learning difficulties, such as confusing letters or numbers, stuttering, or having particular trouble learning to read or write, it's certainly not time to panic. But it might be time to seek qualified professional help. Look at the following lists of signs. If you see several of these signs for an extended period of time, an evaluation can do no harm and may, in fact, offer some relief.

Following are some common warning signs that your child might have a learning disability:

## Preschool

- Speaks later than other children of the same or similar age
- Has problems with pronunciation
- Increases vocabulary slowly
- Has difficulty remembering nursery rhymes or rhyming words
- Has difficulty learning numbers, the alphabet, days of the week, colors, or shapes
- Is exceptionally restless and easily distracted
- Has difficulty following directions
- Has difficulty repeating stories
- Demonstrates slow development of fine motor skills
- Has difficulty interacting with peers

## Kindergarten Through Grade 4

- Is slow to learn the connections between letters and their sounds
- Confuses basic words
- Consistently makes reading or spelling errors such as letter reversals (*b, d*) and inversions (*m, w*) (This is often benign in kindergartners.)
- Transposes number sequences or confuses common arithmetic signs
- Is slow to retain facts
- Is slow to learn new skills
- Has difficulty planning
- Has trouble understanding time

- Has poor coordination; is clumsy or accident prone
- Has difficulty gripping his or her pencil

## Grades 5 Through 8

- Reverses letter sequences (*left*, *felt*)
- Avoids reading aloud
- Has difficulty with handwriting
- Is slow to learn prefixes, suffixes, and so on
- Avoids writing assignments
- Has difficulty recalling facts
- Has difficulty understanding facial expressions and body language
- Has difficulty making friends

## High School Through Adulthood

- Spells poorly
- Frequently spells the same word differently
- Avoids reading and writing whenever possible
- Seems to have weak memory skills
- Is extremely disorganized and forgetful
- Has difficulty adjusting to different surroundings
- Has difficulty grasping abstract concepts
- Works slowly
- Has difficulty summarizing

Most parents are likely to observe one or more of these warning signs in their children at one time or another. As I stated above, this doesn't necessarily suggest a problem. However, if you observe several of these signs for an extended period of time, it may be a good idea to have your child evaluated by a professional who specializes in child development and learning. Even if these signs aren't picked up until adulthood, there are still things that can be done to help.

Depending on the problem, you might wish to seek out a speech and language therapist, a learning specialist, an occupational or physical therapist, or a child psychologist. If the problem is medical or complicated by medical issues, you may want to consult a developmental pediatrician, a pediatric neurologist, a child psychiatrist, or a child neuropsychologist. If you aren't certain who to go to for your child's problems, any of these professionals should be able to help direct you and offer referrals to the proper individuals.

I evaluate many children and adolescents with learning and other neurodevelopmental problems. Whether these problems are mild, moderate, or severe, early intervention is crucial for a child's learning and development if he or she is experiencing problems in school.

## Choosing a Good Child Psychologist

Be very careful when it comes to choosing your child's psychotherapist. Although there may be some financial savings in choosing a therapist who's part of your insurance plan, this should not be the primary consideration. Inquire about the therapist's educational background and credentials. Your child's therapist should have up-to-date knowledge of brain research and an awareness of the current views on the issues such as learning delays, attention problems, and social and emotional problems.

It's also important to ascertain if a therapist has previously worked with children who have needs similar to those of your child. Parents should familiarize themselves with various therapeutic approaches—for example, psychodynamic and behavioral—and feel satisfied that the therapist will use one appropriate to the child's presenting problem. This may mean doing a little more research, but it will undoubtedly be worth any time you invest.

Finally, and perhaps most important, both you and your child should feel comfortable with the therapist and the therapeutic environment. To some degree, you should trust your instincts as well as those of your child.

**Famous Lefty Royalty**

- Alexander the Great
- Charlemagne
- Julius Caesar
- Napoleon Bonaparte
- Joséphine de Beauharnais, Napoleon's first wife
- King Louis XVI of France
- Queen Victoria of England
- King George II of England
- Queen Elizabeth, Queen Mother of England
- King George VI of England
- Queen Elizabeth II of England
- Prince Charles of England
- Prince William of England

# Chapter Ten

# The Gifts of Left-Handedness

## Advantages

Although throughout this book I've focused primarily on dealing with the many obstacles left-handers face, the fact is that they have a great many advantages. Probably the most notable advantage left-handers possess is their resilience and adaptability. Often when the left hand is injured or otherwise occupied, the right hand is eager to take over. Left-handers tend to find ways, both physically and mentally, of dealing with injury, inconvenience, and incapacitation. Quite often, they are more versatile. For instance, when painting a room I can hold the roller in either hand. I don't have to keep moving the ladder around to reach different areas. Of course, house painting is not a crucial skill, but this example gives you an idea of the possibilities.

Left-handers may have better spatial abilities. As I explained in Chapter Eight, this means that lefties may have an enhanced sense of the distances between themselves and other objects, how objects are related in space, and mathematics.

## Special Talents and Skills

Sometimes being different is a positive thing. Music, the visual arts, the sciences, politics, a great variety of competitive sports—this is just a short list of areas where left-handed people seem to excel. Even if we can't prove a direct relationship between left-handedness and the skills required for these varied fields, the anecdotal evidence appears to suggest that there must be some significant advantages to being left-handed.

### Athletic Skills

Baseball is probably the first sport that comes to mind when you think of left-handed athletes. Although there

---

Your child's left-handedness is one of the elements that distinguish him or her and should be a source of pride.

---

is good reason for this, there are numerous other sports at which lefties have consistently excelled. In some sports, such as tennis, where the court is symmetrical, a left-handed player may have an intrinsic edge. Opponents are often forced to make dramatic adjustments to their playing strategies and techniques. The backhand, for instance, is now the forehand. And in baseball, where right-handed players are accustomed to going up against right-handed opponents, lefties present special problems. An inside pitch is outside now. But the fact is that left-handers prosper in almost every sport, including those where they don't play directly against a competitor. This may be because the two sides of the brain are forced to work more closely together in left-handers. Whatever the reasons, it's clear that left-handedness should never be thought of as a handicap in athletic endeavors.

## Creative Skills

There are those who feel left-handers are particularly creative. Though this has never been scientifically proven, there are great numbers of left-handers in every field in which creativity plays a significant role. Indeed, it sometimes seems that there is an excess of left-handed artists, sculptors, dancers, musicians, and writers. Michelangelo, Picasso, Mark Twain, Eudora Welty, James Baldwin, Judy Garland, David Bowie, George Burns, and Natalie Cole are all part of a diverse group of individuals who share a common trait—creativity.

Whether this suggests a pattern is open to debate, but it certainly suggests that left-handers are not lacking in creativity.

But the old notion that left-handers are "right-brained" is erroneous. We are indeed using our right brains for writing and some other motor skills, but this doesn't necessarily mean the right side of a left-hander's brain is dominating the left in other areas.

## Musical Skills

Judging by the number of great left-handed musicians, you might well believe lefties have a special talent for music, particularly when you consider the obstacles they can face. Classical pianists and composers like Beethoven and Carl Philipp Emanuel Bach have been undaunted by right-handed equipment and training; rock guitar legends Robert Plant and Jimi Hendrix have broken musical barriers; and horn players such as Wynton Marsalis and Rich Szabo have demonstrated a proficiency unrivaled by their right-handed contemporaries.

## The Visual Arts

I personally have no artistic skill whatsoever—it's almost as though someone forgot to put a right brain in my head. But when researchers went into graduate schools, they found an unusually high percentage of left-handers in fields such as the graphic arts and architecture. However, I would be cautious about attaching any great significance to these statistics. The fact is that there is a preponderance of left-handers in almost all graduate schools. It may be that more lefties tend to go to graduate school. But then again, it may be that Pablo Picasso, Michelangelo, M. C. Escher, and dozens of other successful left-handed artists shared an intrinsic talent that was in some way related to their lateral preferences. They certainly weren't stifled by them.

## Logic and Intelligence

There is anecdotal evidence that left-handers tend to be more intelligent than righties, but, as much as we might like to believe that, it has never been scientifically proven. It could be that left-handers tend to fall on the extremes regarding intelligence. Rather than a bell-shaped intelligence curve, the line for lefties might be straighter, with greater quantities on both ends. I know that at least 30 to 40 percent of practicing psychologists are left-handed, and I suspect that you could find similar statistics in other areas that require extraordinary academic skills. As I stated earlier, the graduate schools in this country, and probably in others, are teeming with left-handers.

We are all distinct individuals in how we look, how we act, and how our brains function. Still, with company like Benjamin Franklin, Helen Keller, Albert Einstein, Marcia Clark, Henry Ford, Ruth Bader Ginsberg, and Albert Schweitzer, it's hard to believe we don't have some advantage over our right-handed neighbors.

# Differences

## *Ways of Thinking*

Over the years, there has been some research on how left-ies think. Supposedly, their thinking is more multimodal, not as rigid or as strict as the thinking of most righties. The reason for this is that their brains' cognitive functions are wired differently. Skills and abilities that are strictly lateralized to one side of the brain in most right-handers may be diffusely organized in left-handers. Left-handers may have certain cognitive abilities represented on both sides of their brains. If this is true, it would lead to more cooperation and sharing of information between the two hemispheres.

## *Mathematics*

Mathematics is a specialized skill, one that requires a distinctive kind of reasoning. Interestingly, it is widely believed that left-handers have a proclivity for math skills. For several years, Dr. Camilla Benbow and her colleagues at Johns Hopkins University followed preco-cious children with extraordinary math skills. This pro-ject, known as the Mathematically Precocious Youth Project, studied a group of boys who, at the age of 12 or

> Research suggests that lefties' thinking is more multi-modal and not as rigid or strict as that of their right-handed counterparts.

13 scored above 700 on the Quantitative section of the SAT exams. What they found is that the handedness distribution among these children approximated a normal curve rather than a J-shaped curve. This means that their handedness is skewed neither to the right nor to the left, suggesting that these children may lack a right-shift gene factor. Also, the percentage of lefties in this group is much higher than in the normal population. Unfortunately, Dr. Benbow was unable to duplicate this study with left-handed girls, nor did she have enough girls in the sample at the time.

My own experience is that many left-handers are indeed very good in math, but that may be an artifact of the field I'm in. I have also observed that many left-handed girls have poor topographical orientation—difficulty navigating their surroundings and understanding directions. It isn't clear what all of this data means. What is clear is that there is still some work to be done before we fully understand the differences between lefties and righties.

> Lefties may have an enhanced sense of distance, spatial relations, and mathematics.

## Viewing Left-Handedness as a Gift

I suppose we all have the desire to see ourselves as special and unique; we all want to lay claim to some individual gift, something that makes us stand out from the crowd.

If dealt with properly, your child's left-handedness can be one of the elements that distinguishes him or her and brings a sense of pride.

Many left-handers do indeed find a sense of identity in their left-handedness. They know the lists of famous lefties, and they learn the myths, the legends, and the science. What some left-handers don't realize is that their flexibility, their innate ability to adjust more easily to changes in the environment and to perform tasks with either hand, can be a great gift. If they injure one hand, they can generally learn to use the other more easily than can their right-handed brothers and sisters, and as you've seen, they seem to do extremely well in numerous sports, arts, and academic endeavors.

They are indeed different, and in that difference is a part of their identity. Even with the growing awareness of the obstacles they sometimes face, there may be some struggles early on, and there may be occasional misunderstandings. But if managed properly, that needn't do any long-term harm. Certainly, we don't know if your left-handed child will grow up to be a great artist, a renowned musician, a world leader, or a neuropsychologist, but we do know that with loving guidance and thoughtful support, he or she will grow up to be a valuable member of the diverse human family.

> Studies have shown that if a lefty injures his or her dominant hand, he or she can learn to use the other one more easily than can right-handed counterparts.

# Resources

## Web Sites

Note to readers: The following list of Web sites is extensive but may not be complete because new Web sites are built every day, and other Web sites cease to exist just as quickly. That's both the beauty and frustration of modern technology. In addition, many of these Web sites, especially the resource and information sites, will lead you to other new sites. In short, there's a lot going on for lefties on the Internet!

AC2-W.com
Left-handed products and information
www.ac2w.com/en_ac2w.html

Anything Left-Handed
Left-handed products and information
www.anythingleft-handed.co.uk

Arniss Lefthand Bass Guitars
Left-handed guitars
rock.soundcity.de/arni/index.htm

Being Left Handed
Information and opinions
www.his.com/~pshapiro/left.handed.html

Being Left-Handed, by E. Stephen Mack
Information, discussion, and resources, including a simple explanation for elementary school students of what it's like to be a lefty
www.emf.net/~estephen/facts/lefthand.html

Colorado Boomerangs
Left-handed equipment and gifts
www.coloradoboomerangs.com/howto/

European's Left-Handers Page
Information and resources
www.linkshaenderseite.de/english.html

For Southpaws Only, by Janis Cortese
Information, opinion, and resources
www.io.com/~cortese/left/southpaw.html

Gauche, by M. K. Holder
A very comprehensive site of information, opinion, and resources
www.indiana.edu/~primate/lspeak.html

Human Left-Handedness, by Lam Wai-Hang
Information, opinion, and resources
pages.nyu.edu/~whl203/lefty/lefty.html

The Left Hand Drive Place
Over 100 left-hand-drive cars
www.lhdplace.co.uk

The Left-Hand.com
Left-handed tools, including left-handed corkscrews
with reversed coils
www.thelefthand.com/h405406.htm

Left-handed.com
Left-handed products and information
www.left-handed.com

Left-handed BAA/NBA/ABA Players
Left-handed sports players
members.aol.com/apbrhist/lefties.html

Left Hand Education
Left-handed products and information
www.lefthand-education.co.uk

Left Hand Publishing
Information, resources, and a newsletter
www.lefthandpublishing.com

The Left-handed Writers Page
Left-handed products and information, especially pens
and other writing implements
www.nibs.com/Left-hand%20writers.html

Lefty, The Original Left Handed Guitar Chord Book
Chords for lefty guitarists
people.enternet.com.au/~lefty/index.html

Lefty's Book Store
Books for and about lefties
people.enternet.com.au/~lefty/leftybks.html

Leftportside.com
Left-handed products
www.leftyportside.com

Loren's Left-Handed Site
Information, opinions, and resources
duke.usask.ca/~elias/left

Molly Joy's Left-Handedness Page
Information, opinion, and resources
www.geocities.com/Athens/Acropolis/1684/lefthand.
html

National Association of Left-Handed Golfers
Association for lefty golfers
www.nalg.org

Northern California Left Handed Golfer's Association
Association for lefty golfers
www.leftygolf.org

New England Computer Supply
Left-handed keyboards, left-handed mouse devices,
assistive technology, and products for disabled needs;
company also has a retail store in Massachusetts—see
page 162 for address
www.ergosupply.com/detail.html

Rik Smits' Lefthanded Universe
Information, opinions, products, and resources
www.xs4all.nl/~riksmits/lhu/lhu.html

Rosemary West's Left-Handed Page
Information, opinions, and resources
www.rosemarywest.com/left

Southpaw Enterprises
Left-handed products, including a reasonably priced circular saw
www.southpaw.bc.ca

## Shops, Retailers, Wholesalers, Mail Order

*United States*

### California

Left Handed World of Carmel, Inc.
Vanderfort Court (San Carlos at 7th)
P.O. Box 7222
Carmel-by-the-Sea, CA 93921

Left Hand World
P.O. Box 330128
Pier 39
San Francisco, CA 94111
Phone: (415) 433-3547

Lefty, Inc.
P.O. Box 1054
Torrence, CA 90505

The Left Hand Supply Company
P.O. Box 20188
Oakland, CA 94620-0188
Phone: (510) 658-LEFT
Fax: (510) 655-7612

The Southpaw Shoppe
849 West Harbor Drive, suite B
San Diego, CA 92101
Phone: (619) 239-1731

The Left-Handed Compliment
11359 Bolas Street
Los Angeles, CA 90049

The Lefty Shop
7008 S Washington Avenue
Whittier, CA 90602

Route 66 Guitars
3579 E. Foothill Boulevard, #321
Pasadena, CA 91107
Phone/fax: (213) GUITARS (484-8277)
E-mail: lefty@southpaw.com
www.southpaw.com

The Southpaw Shoppe
849 West Harbor Drive, suite B
San Diego, CA 92101
Phone: (619)239-1731
A $1 catalogue can be requested from
P.O. Box 2870
San Diego, CA 92112

## Connecticut

The Artistera Organization
9 Rices Lane
P.O. Box 647
Westport, CT 06880

## Delaware

What's Left
"Left-handed Cards for Right-minded People"
P.O. Box 829
Bear, DE 19701-0829
Send self-addressed, stamped envelope for a listing of card lines offered.

## Florida

The Left-Hand Shoppe
Amtel Mall #4312
2855 Colonial Boulevard
Fort Myers, FL 33912 *and*
2609 5th St. W
Lehigh Acres, FL 33971
Phone: (941)277-7022
E-mail: lefty@iline.com
www.wh4.com/lefty

Southpaw Solutions
Lefty/Portside
P.O. Box 543
Hernando, FL 34442
Phone: (800)245-LEFT (-5338)
www.leftyportside.com

## Georgia

Sweet Pea's Shoppe
P.O. Box 80595
Conyers, GA 30013
Phone: (770) 922-1390

## Illinois

Left Hand Plus, Inc.
P.O. Box 161
Morton Grove, IL 60053

## Massachusetts

Left Hand Compliments
P.O. Box 647
Brookline Village, MA 02147

Lefthanded Compliments
241 Perkins Street, suite I-302
Jamaica Plain, MA 02130
Phone: (617) 232-2822 or (800) 676-5338
Fax: (617) 735-1833

New England Computer Supply
89 North Main Street
P.O. Box 1991
Andover, MA 01810
Left-handed keyboards, mouse devices, assistive technology, and products for disabled needs; you can also order from the Web site
Phone: (978) 474-0088
Fax: (978) 474-0085

E-mail: necs@ergosupply.com
www.ergosupply.com

## New Mexico

Truly Yours—Lefty Section
1439 Eubank Boulevard, NE
Albuquerque, NM 87112
Phone: (800) 474-6172
Fax: (505) 332-7972
www.trulyyours.com/lefty.htm

## Michigan

Lefties Corner
508 Monroe
Detroit, MI 48226
Phone: (313) 964-5123

## Missouri

Lefty Lane Gifts
104 N. Commercial Street
Branson, MO 65616
Phone: (417) 336-3920
Fax: (417) 337-7624
www.leftylane.com

## New York

The Left-Hand Shoppe
8806 Honeycomb Path
Cicero, NY 13039
Phone: (800) 390-1048

Fax: (315) 699-3910
www.cybermall2.com/lefty

Leftporium
P.O. Box 609
Monticello, NY 12701
Free catalog on request
Phone: (914) 791-7991
Fax: (914) 791-1062
E-mail: lefty1@warwick.net
www.leftporium.com

Left Hand Solutions and Registry Inc.
P.O. Box 617
Port Jefferson Station, NY 11776
Phone: (631) 474-0091

The Left Hand
140 W. 22nd Street
New York, NY 10011

Southpaw's Serenity
P.O. Box 290565
Brooklyn, NY 11229-0565
Phone: (718) 769-3354
Fax: (718) 769-4284

## Ohio

Handtiques
6072 Busch Boulevard
Columbus, OH 43229
Phone: (614) 846-0778

## Oregon

The SouthPaw
5331 SW Macadam Ave.
Portland, OR 97201

## Pennsylvania

Lefty's Corner
P.O. Box 615
Department EM
Clarks Summit, PA 18411
Phone: (717) 586-5338
Catalogue: Send $2.00 (refundable with first order)

The Left Hand
P.O. Box 3263
Bethlehem, PA 18017-2063
Phone: (800) 462-5338 or (610) 923-0677
Fax: (610) 923-0678
www.thelefthand.com

## Texas

Fry's Left-Handers Supply
P.O. Box 19, Country Ridge
Melissa, TX 75071
Phone: (214) 871-0719

Southpaw Guitars
5813 Bellaire Boulevard
Houston, TX 77081
Phone: (713) 667-5791

## Vermont

Lefties Only Golf
1972 Williston Road S.
Burlington, VT 05403
Phone: (800) LEFTIES (533-8437); outside United States, (802) 862-1114
E-mail: leftiesonlygolf@msn.com

## Wisconsin

Left Handed Limited
433 W. Silver Spring Drive
Milwaukee, WI 53217

## *Canada*

## Alberta

Left-Hand Advantage
60 William Bell Drive
Leduc, Alberta, Canada
T9E 6N8
Phone: (800) 683-5507 or (403) 986-6104
Fax: (800) 249-4699 or (403) 986-4704

## British Columbia

Southpaw Enterprises
P.O. Box 835
Nelson, British Columbia, Canada
V1L 5P5
Phone: (800) 818-9616

Resources

www.worldtel.com/netidea/southpaw/southpaw.htm
and, coming soon, www.southpaw.bc.ca/home.htm

## Ontario

Johnathan's Ledge: The Lefty Haven
The Royal Hotel
102 Metcalfe Street
Elora, Ontario, Canada
N0B 1S0
Phone: (519) 846-8500

Left Hand Products
1920 Ellesmere Road, suite 104-252
Scarborough, Ontario, Canada
M1H 3G1
Phone: (416) 439-2199
Fax: (416) 289-3321 or (800) 561-0411 (North
America–wide)
E-mail: lefty@sentex.net

The Sinister Shop
P.O. Box 261, Station C
Toronto, Ontario, Canada
M6J 2P4
Phone: (416) 366-1790

## Quebec

La Boutique des Gauchers
26 Rue De'ry
St-Stanislas, Quebec, Canada
G0X 3E0
Phone: (418) 328-4485 or (418) 328-8629

The Left Hander
P.O. Box 211
N.D.G. Station
Montreal, Quebec, Canada
H4A 3P5

## *International*

Anything Left Handed, Ltd.
Left-handed gadgets; mail order available
65 Beak Street
P.O. Box 45L
London, England
WIA 45SL

AXCI
Box 563
S-236 25 Hollviken
Sweden
Phone: 46 (0)40-45 09 04

De Dreta a Esquerra
Copernic 85
08021 Barcelona, Spain
Phone/fax: +34-(9) 3-201 93 92
E-mail: lefty@solution4u.com, zurdos@solution4u.com
English: www.geocities.com/Eureka/Plaza/8220/
Spanish: www.geocities.com/Eureka/Plaza/8221/

Left Handed Products
Box 5189 G.P.O.
N.S.W. 2001
Sydney, Australia

ZURDOandia
Cl Bolonia, 10 (Esq. Cte. Sta. Pau)
50008—Zaragoza, Spain
Phone: (976) 22-63-80
Fax: (976) 22-63-80

## Organizations

National Association of Left-Handed Golfers
P.O. Box 801223
Houston, TX 77280-1223
Phone: (713) 464-8683

Sinistral SIG
(A lefties-only division of Mensa)
200 Emmett Avenue
Derby, CT 06418
Phone: (203) 735-1759

Left Handers International
Ms. Nancy Campbell,
Executive Director
3601 SW 29th Street
Topeka, KS 66614

League of Lefthanders
Mike and Tom Geden
P.O. Box 495
Maple Shade, NJ 08052
E-mail: leagueoflefthanders@bigfoot.net

# Books

*Best Friends, Hands Down*
by Terry Wolfe Phelan and Marilyn Hafner
Shoe Tree Press, June 1986, $9.95
Children's book about lefties

*Calligraphy: The Italic Alphabet for Right and Left-Handed Writers*
by Mary Jane Gormley
Ink Spot Press, $8.95, paperback
Instructional book

*The Dominance Factor: How Knowing Your Dominant Eye, Ear, Brain, Hand & Foot Can Improve Your Learning*
by Carla Hannaford, Ph.D.
Great Ocean Publishers, April 1997, $14.95, paperback

*Hemispheric Asymmetry: What's Right and What's Left*
by Joseph B. Hellige
Harvard University Press, March 2001, $16.95, paperback
Considers the biology of asymmetry; scientific

*Left-Handed Calligraphy*
by Vance Studley
Dover Publications, June 1991, $3.95, paperback
Instructional and illustrated

*The Left-Hander Syndrome: The Causes and Consequences of Left-Handedness*
by Stanley Coren
Vintage Books, July 1993, $14.00, trade paperback
The history, anthropology, and neurobiology of left-handedness

*Left-Handed Sewing*
by Sally Cowan
Dover Publications, February 1994, $2.95, paperback
Instructional

*Left Is Right: The Survival Guide for Living Lefty in a Right-Handed World*
by Rae Lindsay
Gilmour House, September 1996, $9.95, paperback

*The Left-Hander's Guide to Life*
by Richard Donley and Leigh W. Rutledge; illustrated by James Bennett
Plume, August 1992, $9.95, paperback
A lighthearted look at left-handedness

*Left-Handed Kids*
by James T. De Kay
M. Evans & Co., October 1989, $5.95
Children's book for lefties

*Left-Handed Shortstop*
by Patricia Reilly Giff
Econo-Clad Books, October 1999, $11.10, paperback
Children's novel about a left-handed ball player

*The Natural Superiority of the Left-Hander*
by James T. De Kay
M. Evans & Co, September 1979, $3.95, paperback

*The World's Greatest Left-Handers: Why Left-handers Are Just Plain Better Than Everybody Else*
by James T. De Kay and Sandy Huffaker
M. Evans & Co, July 1989, $5.95, paperback
Famous lefties in history

# Newsletter

*Left-Handers Newsletter*
Left Hand Publishing
P.O. Box 438
Farmington, MI 48332-0438
Phone: (800) 511-5338
Fax: (248) 615-3501
E-mail: info@lefthandpublishing.com

# Bibliography

## General References

Annett, Marian. *Left, Right, Hand and Brain: The Right Shift Theory.* Hillsdale, New Jersey: Lawrence Erlbaum, 1985.

## Chapter One

de Kay, James T. *The Natural Superiority of the Left-Hander.* New York: M. Evans and Company, 1979.
Healy, Jane M. *Your Child's Growing Mind: A Guide to Learning and Brain Development from Birth to Adolescence.* New York: Doubleday, 1987.

## Chapter Two

Annett, M. *Left, Right, Hand and Brain: The Right Shift Theory.* Hillsdale, New Jersey: Lawrence Erlbaum, 1985.

Burnham, Janine. *Parent Guide*. June 1997.

Corballis, Michael. Symposium on Human Handedness. The 28th annual meeting of the International Neuropsychological Society, Denver, Colorado. February 2000.

Coren, Stanley. *The Left-Hander Syndrome: The Causes and Consequences of Left-Handedness*. New York: Vintage Books, 1993.

Geschwind, Norman, and Galaburda, Albert. *Cerebral Lateralization: Biological Mechanisms, Associations, and Pathology*. Cambridge, Massachusetts: MIT Press, 1987.

Healey, J. M., Liederman, J., and Geschwind, N. Handedness Is Not a Unidimensional Trait. *Cortex* 22:32–53, 1986.

Liederman, J., and Healey, J. M. Independent Dimensions of Hand Preference: Reliability of the Factor Structure and the Handedness Inventory. *Archives of Clinical Neuropsychology* 1:371–386, 1986.

McManus, Chris. Symposium on Human Handedness. The 28th annual meeting of the International Neuropsychological Society, Denver, Colorado. February 2000.

Perelle, I. B., and Ehrman, L. An International Study of Human Handedness: The Data. *Behavioral Genetics* 24, 217–227, 1994.

Porac, Clare, and Coren, Stanley. *Lateral Preferences and Human Behavior*. New York: Springer-Verlag, 1977.

Singh, M., and Bryden, M. P. The Factor Structure of Handedness in India. *International Journal of Neuroscience* 74:33–43, 1994.


# Chapter Three

Annett, Marian. *Left, Right, Hand and Brain: The Right Shift Theory.* Hillsdale, New Jersey: Lawrence Erlbaum, 1985.

Bryden, M. P. Measuring Handedness with Questionnaires. *Neuropsychologia* 15:617–624, 1979.

Dean, R. S. Assessing Patterns of Lateral Preference. *Journal of Clinical Neuropsychology* 4:124–128, 1982.

Dean, Raymond S., and Reynolds, Cecil R. Cognitive Processing and Self-Report of Lateral Preference. *Neuropsychology Review* 7(3):127–142, 1997.

Liederman, J. Mechanisms Underlying Discontinuities in the Development of Handedness. In G. Young, S. J. Segalowitz, C. Corter, and S. Trehub (eds.), *Manual Specialization and the Developing Brain* (pp. 71–92). New York: Academic Press, 1983.

Steenhuis, R. E., and Bryden, M. P. Different Dimensions of Hand Preference That Relate to Skilled and Unskilled Activities. *Cortex* 25:289–304, 1989.

# Chapter Four

Bakan, P., Dibb, G. and Reed, P. Handedness and Birth Stress. *Neuropsychologia* 3:363–366, 1973.

Bradshaw, J. L. *Hemispheric Specialization and Psychological Function.* Chichester: Wiley, 1989.

Bryden, M. P. *Laterality: Functional Asymmetry in the Intact Brain.* New York: Academic Press, 1982.

Corballis, M. C. *Human Laterality.* New York: Academic Press, 1983.

Diamond, S., and Beaumont, J. *Hemisphere Function in the Human Brain.* London: Elek Scientific Books, 1974.

Gazzaniga, M. S. *The Bisected Brain.* New York: Appleton-Century-Crofts, 1970.

Geschwind, N. *Selected Papers on Language and the Brain.* The Netherlands: D. Reidel Publishing Company, 1974.

Geschwind, N., and Levitsky, W. Human Brain: Left–Right Asymmetries in Temporal Speech Region. *Science* 161:186–187, 1968.

Goodglass, H., and Quadfasel, F. A. Language Laterality in Left-Handed Aphasics. *Brain* 77:521–548, 1954.

Levy, J. Lateral Specialization of the Human Brain: Behavioral Manifestations and Possible Evolutionary Basis. In Kriger, J. (ed.), *The Biology of Behavior.* Corvallis, Oregon: Oregon State University Press, 1973.

Satz, P. Pathological Left-Handedness: An Explanatory Model. *Cortex* 8:121–135, 1972.

## Chapter Five

Levy, J., and Reid, M. Variations in Writing Posture and Cerebral Organization. *Science* 194:337–339, 1976.

Orton, S. T. Specific Reading Disability—Strephosymbolia. *Journal of the American Medical Association* 90:1095–1099, 1937.

Rudel, R. G., Healey, J. M. and Denckla, M. B. Development of Motor Coordination in Normal Left-Handed Children. *Developmental Medicine and Child Neurology* 27:221–233, 1984.

## Chapter Seven

Cavey, Diane W. *Dysgraphia: Why Johnny Can't Write,* 2nd ed. Austin, Texas: Pro-ed, 1987.

Zaner-Bloser, Inc. Catalog. (800) 421-3018.

## Chapter Eight

Bever, T. G. and Chiarello, R. S. Cerebral Dominance in Musicians and Nonmusicians. *Science* 186:537–539, 1974.

## Chapter Ten

Galaburda, A. Developmental Dyslexia: Current Anatomical Research. *Annals of Dyslexia* 33:41–53, 1983.

Hynd, G. W., Marshall, R. M., and Semrud-Clikeman, M. Developmental Dyslexia, Neurolinguistic Theory Deviations in Brain Morphology. *Reading and Writing: An Interdisciplinary Journal* 3:345–362, 1991.

Hynd, G. W., and Semrud-Clikeman, M. Dyslexia and Brain Morphology. *Psychological Bulletin* 106:447–482, 1989.